# THE FAITH-REST LIFE

*By*

**R. B. THIEME, JR., Th.M.**

❧ ❧ ❧
❧ ❧ ❧

# CONTENTS

# THE FAITH-REST LIFE

Our subject, the Faith-Rest Life, will be based upon four passages of Scripture: Exodus 17, Numbers 20 and Hebrews 3 and 4. The first three passages will describe the principles of faith-rest, while Hebrews 4 will analyze the mechanics of it.

## THE PRINCIPLES OF THE FAITH-REST LIFE

We hear much today about the sound barrier. At one time it was considered impossible to fly faster than the speed of sound. Now scientific progress has made this possible, and man has at last "cracked" the sound barrier; he has advanced beyond that point which he thought he could not go. But there is another barrier which poses a problem for the believer, which I like to call the "faith barrier." It takes a great deal of speed to crack the sound barrier, but to crack the faith barrier requires, not excessive speed, but simply standing still. There is no work, no movement involved at all—just believing, or trusting the Lord, keep on trusting Him, and keep waiting on Him. This is a wonderful technique provided experientially for every believer.

We should already know that there is a wonderful place positionally for every believer, for everyone who is "in Christ." "There is therefore now no condemnation to them who are in Christ Jesus" (Romans 8:1). We know that we are new creatures in Christ. We are "bone of His bone and flesh of His flesh." We are partakers of the divine nature. We share the life of Christ, which is eternal life. We share the righteousness of Christ, which is a perfect righteousness. We share His destiny. We share His heir-ship. We share His Sonship. We share His election. We share His Priesthood, and many other things. We know we have a perfect position in Jesus Christ. But I wonder if we realize all that God has provided for us experientially? We are so busy seeking happiness, we are so busy hustling around trying to find something that will satisfy, that we ignore one of the great things in the Word of God—a place of perfect peace! A place of joy (inner happiness)! A place of strength! A place of stability! A place of power! A place of impact! No matter what happens, no matter how difficult the circumstances, no matter how great the pressure, adversities or the problems of life, we can have this "peace of God which passes all understanding" (Philippians 4:7). Or, as someone once quipped, "The peace of God which passes all mis-understanding." So, there is a place of perfect peace, a place of power, a place where our lives can count for Him. Sometimes, the Scripture refers to it as the "Sabbath"—not a seventh day, not a Sabbatical year, but a moment-by-moment Sabbath. It is a place of rest, a place of blessing and of power in the midst of the great adversities of life. It makes possible perfect inner peace in the presence of outer tribulation. It is described for us in the four passages which we will examine in this study.

## THE FIRST MERIBAH INCIDENT
### Exodus 17

In Exodus, chapter 17, we come to a crisis in the history of the Children of Israel. They have been delivered from the bondage of Egypt through the shed blood of the Passover lamb. Having passed through the Red Sea by God's miraculous grace, now Israel faces that vital issue which every believer must sooner or later face in his or her life: If I as a believer, as one who has trusted in Christ and is born again, have trusted Christ for the big thing, which is salvation, can I trust Him for the needs, the problems and the difficulties arising in everyday life? I have trusted Him for the greatest manifestation of His grace. Can I trust Him to graciously meet the problems, the difficulties and the situations which exist daily in my life? Does the Lord really have an answer?

The average minister hears during the course of a week sometimes as many as fifty people relate to him various facets of that which we call "bad news." Now a man could not stay in the ministry unless he had an answer for all of this bad news. If there were no real answer for all the heartaches, the problems, the adversities, the frustrations, the difficulties and the troubles, no minister could stand it for very long. A good many have actually left the ministry simply because they have become so depressed or upset from hearing nothing but troubles. When everything is going right, people do not come to the minister. About the only time people seek a minister when they are happy is when they want to get married. Consequently, a minister hears very little good news from his congregation. However, if he is a minister of the Word, and if he has any concept of the Word, he knows there is a technique in God's Word which provides an answer for every problem, every difficulty and every adverse situation in life, no matter what it is, or how great it is. This is his consolation, this is his blessing and great joy, that no matter what the situation, he has the answer.

However, the mistake so many make is that they want a pat "yes or no" answer to their particular problem. They want the preacher to tell them which way to jump—to say, "turn 90 degrees to the starboard and 3 degrees to the port, and your problem is solved." Yet it is seldom that the minister can outline a specific diagram which says, "do this and this," because before there can be a diagram outlining a certain thing in a certain way, there is a principle which must be followed, and this principle is the solution to ANY problem that any believer will ever face. Now, remember, as you face your problems, the greatest problem in your life has been solved. It was solved at Calvary's cross, for Jesus Christ, "who knew no sin was made sin for you, that you might be made the righteousness of God in him" (II Cor. 5:21). Jesus Christ bore every sin that you have ever committed, solving the sin problem completely. When you trusted in the Son of God, when you received Him as your Lord and Saviour, your sins, positionally, past, present and future, were all blotted out. You entered into a relationship with God for eternity as well as time. And, while you may understand the repercussions of your eternal relationship, it is also important to know the repercussions of your temporal relationship with Him. There are certain experiences which belong to you. There is a fellowship which you can have with the Lord in time, in your every day life. There is a way in which you can honor Him and represent Him. There is a way in which your life can count for Him. It makes no difference who you are or what you are or how discouraged you may be, as long as you are still alive, God has a purpose for your life. God has a reason for your continuance on the face of this earth. He wants you to glorify Him, and He wants you to fulfill your responsibility as an ambassador. You and I face exactly the same issue that the Children of Israel faced many hundreds of years ago. Their problem touched each one of them personally. The Holy Spirit has seen fit to record for us, through the pen of Moses, what to them was an overwhelming situation, although in the light of their great deliverance from Egypt, actually it was not much of a problem at all.

Exodus 17:1. "And all the congregation of the Children of Israel journeyed from the wilderness of Sin, after their journeys, according to the commandment of the Lord. . . ." Notice that the Lord LED them to this place; they were in the Lord's will when they arrived here: "According to the commandment of the Lord." Have you ever been deluded by that evangelistic pitch, "Accept Christ, and you will never have trouble again?" Nothing could be further from the truth. In fact, the opposite is more often the case. "In the world ye shall have tribulation," Christ said. "But be of good cheer; I have overcome the world. These things I have spoken unto you, that in me ye might have peace" (John 16:33). The point is that when you accept Christ, although you possess eternal life and will live in the presence of God forever in your resurrection body, yet you *will* have trouble in time, but you will also have the means of stabilizing and the means of meeting every problem and every difficulty with peace. You haven't lived as a Christian until you have been in a place where you are helpless, where the brook is dried up (I Kings 17:7), where there is no human solution, where there is nothing that you can do or say, where you are so numb from the shock of pressure that you can't even pray! You haven't lived until you have been in that place. For sooner or later God brings every believer to the "dried-up brook." And every believer must face a set of circumstances where the situation is black and hopeless, where there is no human solution. That is exactly what God did with the Children of Israel.

At this point He has delivered them from the bondage of Egypt, He has led them through the water of the Red Sea, and they have now moved to the place called Rephidim. Here in this wilderness there was no water for the people to drink. A great

host of people—perhaps as many as two million adults, plus all of
their children—and not one drop of water! The Hebrew word for
wilderness is "desert." Just wasteland! Dry sand! Though led by
God to a dry desert place, they face a very serious water problem.
Quickly they begin to suffer. Now God permitted this for one purpose. God is saying to that generation, as He is saying to us as
believers today, "Will you trust Me?"

"He that spared not His own Son, but delivered Him up for
us all, how shall He not with Him also freely give us all things"
(Romans 8:32). You have trusted Him for Salvation. You have
believed in Jesus Christ and have received Him as your Lord and
Saviour. That was the greatest thing He ever did for you, for it
cost Him infinitely more to send His Son to the cross to die for
your sins than anything else He could have done. If He did the
most for you at Calvary's cross, will He do less for you now? If He
did the most for you when you were His enemy, and we were all
His enemies when Christ died for us (Romans 5:10), what will
He do for you now that you are His son? Can He do less than He
did before? Emphatically not! He will do more. But there is only
one thing that God required for them to enter into this moment-by-
moment Sabbath, the place of perfect peace and stability. Faith!
He says, "Trust Me, will you?" For this very purpose He has given
us promises in writing, promises we can take by faith and use and
believe, promises which will stabilize the believer.

Now in the passage before us, there is an opportunity for a
people in a desperate situation to avail themselves of God's provision, to enter into His perfect rest. I wish I could read in verse 2
words like this:

> So the people all knelt down and said,
> 'thank you Lord for giving us this tremendous
> opportunity to trust Thee. And, while the out-
> look is black, we have the uplook and we await
> Thy pleasure right here. We trust Thee right
> here for water, and we are simply waiting now
> to see Thee work. We recognize that Moses
> said on the other side of the Red Sea, Stand still
> and watch the deliverance of the Lord, and we
> stood there and we watched. Now we stand
> still again to watch Thee work.'

Wouldn't that be wonderful? Well, I wouldn't have much of a sermon if that were true. Certainly it is seldom true of us experientially. How often do we hit the "panic button" when things go wrong? How often do we stay on the wrong side of the faith barrier? How often do we get upset and fall apart and get disturbed? Yet, if there are any people on the face of the earth who ought to be calm and courageous, exhibiting peace with joy and strength and impact in the midst of adversity, it ought to be every person who knows Jesus Christ as Lord and Saviour.

*Verse 2.* But instead we read, "Wherefore the people did chide. . . ." Since transliteration is used in most of these passages, I am going to change the word "chide" to its Hebrew word, "Meribah." Hence, the people "Meribahed." Now, today the word "chide" does not mean much. In the day of Shakespeare and in the day of King James, this word would be similar to our modern English word "gripe," or "complain," or "criticize." But we will use the word "Meribah" for reasons you will understand further on.

The people "Meribahed" with Moses. They criticized him, they complained to him, they hit the "panic button" in his presence. They cried, "Give us water that we may drink!" Now what a strange request to Moses. What did they think Moses was going to do? Did they think he would wave a handkerchief in the air and say "Hocus-pocus, where the handkerchief falls we dig a well?" Did they think that Moses had some supernatural power? The deliverance was of the Lord, and Moses had always said so. But this follows the pattern of the old sin nature. When things were going good, Moses never received any credit. When things were going wrong, Moses always was blamed. Human nature must have a scapegoat, and the scapegoat is always the leader. Moses is now beginning to bear that extraordinary pressure that he will carry all of his life, the tremendous pressure of leadership. Here we see Moses with broad shoulders.

"And Moses said unto them, why chide ye with me? (Why do you Meribah with me?) wherefore do ye tempt the Lord (that is, tempt the Lord to take you right out of this life)?" Is the Lord too small for us? Can't the Lord meet our needs? Who was it who delivered us from the hopeless bondage of Egypt? If the Lord did the most for us there, do you think the Lord, Who held back the waters of the Red Sea, could perhaps meet our need of water?

*Verse 3.* The people thirsted there for water. It was a very real thing, a very real problem. The people "Meribahed" against Moses and said, "Wherefore is this that thou hast brought us up out of Egypt to kill us and our children and our cattle with thirst?" In the time of crisis there is always the crowd who complains. Yet, God never intended for any believer to complain in a time of crisis. God intended for every believer to trust Him, to mix the promises of God with faith! To crack the faith barrier! When we complain and when we criticize in the time of crisis and in the time of pressure, we are demonstrating once again our unbelief, our failure to trust Him. Everything that follows in this passage, after such an attitude on the part of God's people, is strictly a matter of GRACE. Some people never see the grace of God, even though they have appropriated it by faith at Calvary's cross. Is it not astounding that God always gives us what we do not deserve, what we cannot earn? And God is going to give water to this people, though they have done nothing to deserve or merit it. They have done everything not to deserve it. While everyone is giving Moses, as we might say, "static," what did this servant of the Lord do?

*Verses 4 and 5.* "Moses cried unto the Lord." Here is a picture of a great man. Moses did not enter into rebuttal. Moses did not enter into argumentation. Moses did not even try to justify himself. He cried to the Lord, saying, "What shall I do unto this people? They be almost ready to stone me."

"And the Lord said unto Moses, Go on before the people. . . ." This is a most interesting answer. The people are ready to stone Moses, yet the Lord says, "get out in front of them where you will make a good target." Now Moses must obey the Lord and go before these people who have their hands filled with rocks, but how is he going to do it? Is he going out there in the courage of his own strength? No, he is going to walk out there like David before the giant. Moses believed the Lord in the crisis! That is why Moses was the leader. The others could criticize, complain and shout their imprecations, but they did not have that quiet, stable, strong, steady quality as did Moses, which could trust the Lord moment by moment. Moses believed it when he said, "The Lord will fight for you today" (Exodus 14:13), or as David expressed it, "The battle is the Lord's" (I Sam. 17:47). Thus, Moses obeyed his Commanding Officer and went before the angry mob whose hands were filled with stones. Then the Lord added, "And take with thee the elders of Israel. . . ." In other words, "Moses, since there are others who will share the leadership responsibilities, and who need to learn to trust Me, get them out there so they too can be a target for the rocks of the people."

". . . and thy rod, wherewith thou smotest the river, take in thine hand, and go." This is a special rod. This is a rod of judgment.

*Verse 6.* Now follows a promise from the Lord. "Behold, I will stand before thee there upon the rock. . . ." The Hebrew word for rock is a sharp, jagged rock. Here we see a type, as well as a record of historical truth. It is a picture of Christ the Rock, being smitten for us on Calvary's cross (I Cor. 10:4). For just as Moses would take the rod in his hand and would strike the jagged rock, so God the Father smote God the Son on Calvary's cross for you and for me, and as a result, from Christ comes the water of salvation.

"Behold, I will stand before thee there upon the rock in Horeb; and thou shalt smite the rock, and there shall come water out of it, that the people may drink." Now notice the obedience of faith. Moses did exactly as the Lord instructed him. "Moses did so in the sight of the elders of Israel. And he called the name of the place Massah, and Meribah." Will you please remember the Meribah? If I should say to you as good Texans, "Remember the Alamo!" you would know exactly what I meant. Now I say to you as a believer in the Lord Jesus Christ, "Remember the Meribah!" Remember the warning of unbelief, of failure to crack the faith barrier!

# THE SECOND MERIBAH INCIDENT
## NUMBERS 20

After 40 years of wandering, after the generation of the Exodus has died off, a new generation of the Children of Israel come back to the same place where their fathers had been tested with no water. Would they remember the Meribah?

*Verse 1.* "Then came the children of Israel, even the whole congregation, into the desert of Zin in the first month. . . ." (Now in verse 2, the same test in the same spot). "And there was no water for the congregation. . . ." What has happened during that 40 years? During that 40 years the Children of Israel have had many pressures, many problems, many needs, and all during that time God had graciously and faithfully provided every need that the Jews had for their wilderness journey. If they needed shoes, and they did, He supplied them. If they needed water, and they did, He supplied it. If they needed knowledge of military science for their enemies, He supplied it. If they needed food, and they did, He supplied it. He met every need they had for 40 years. For 40 years the Children of Israel had seen nothing but the faithfulness of God!

I want this to be practical to you, even though it happened many centuries ago. Put in the place of "no water" whatever your problem is right now. No what? No money? No friends? No happiness? No husband? No wife? What is it? There is a "no something" in everyone's life, but that "no something" has a purpose. God has a reason for it, and He says to you through that "no something" you think you lack, "Will you trust Me? I have given you something that I did not give that generation in the wilderness. I have given you over 7,000 promises for time—and in writing." When God says it, that settles it. When He writes it, that clinches it! "The Word of God liveth and abideth forever" (I Peter 1:23). As eternal God, as Sovereign, as undiminished deity, as omnipotent—yes, with all of His omnipotence, God does not have the power to go back on His Word. Have you ever thought of that? He cannot go back on His Word! However, these 7,000 promises can only be used in time. You cannot take them with you. There are many promises for eternity, such as Philippians 3:21, where we are promised a body like the Son of God; Revelation 21:4, "There shall be no more death, neither sorrow, nor crying, neither shall there be any more pain; for the former things are passed away." There is the promise in heaven of a mansion (John 14:2), and of being "face to face with the Lord" (II Corinthians 5:8).

But we are now dealing with time, with the "no water" problem; with the situation that you face right now, for we are a people with no water, although the "no water" is different in every case. Every one of us has a problem. Every one of us faces some difficult situation. If you think you have no problems, just rest assured, you will sooner or later. Even though you are in a place of prosperity now, you would do well to take heed to God's warning, for prosperity also has its problems. When things are going smoothly, it is often more difficult to keep your eyes on the Lord than during adversity. Too, we must remember that prosperity does not always last. Adversity is pretty certain at some time in your life. Yet even in suffering and pressure, it is possible to possess the same joy, the same peace and blessing which you had in prosperity. This is the stability which is produced by continuous faith, no matter what the circumstances. Faith must be tested through pressure so that we will mature and so that we will learn to lean upon Him. You and I have in writing all that we need to pass the test. We simply claim it by faith. The Children of Israel had the chance to "crack the faith barrier," to pass the test of faith in Numbers 20, at the same place where the first generation failed.

*Verses 2 and 3.* "There was no water for the congregation: and they gathered themselves together against Moses and against Aaron. And the people chode (Meribahed) with Moses, and spake, saying, Would God that we had died when our brethren died before the Lord!"

This is a familiar complaint. I have heard it so many times and in so many ways. "Oh, I wish I were dead. Life is so hard!" This is Elijah crawling under the juniper tree. I have often thought that if there were some way to scare these people into thinking they were going to die in about a second, they would change in a hurry. "I wish I were dead. Lord, let me die. No one has it as rough as I have it." It is interesting to observe that often the people who say this say it to someone who is having a much more difficult time than they are. Now, listen to the congregation in the wilderness, "Would God we had died when our brethren died."

They didn't want to die when their brethren died. Why, their brethren had died the sin unto death—believers who died because they had failed the Lord so often and so long that God removed them out of the world. It is much like a star quarterback saying to himself, "Oh, I wish the coach would jerk me!" Why, he doesn't want to be jerked out of the game. If he has failed, he wants to keep going and try to rectify his mistakes. Who ever heard of a football player wanting the coach to take him out of the game just because he has made a mistake? He wants to stay in there and he wants to keep going. I don't know why it is, but believers so often get to this place and then say, "I wish I were dead."

*Verses 4 and 5.* These people had fallen into this same pattern, and so they said, "Why have ye brought up the congregation of the Lord into this desert place, that we and our cattle should die there? And wherefore have ye made us to come up out of Egypt, to bring us into the evil place?"

Now they are saying that Moses made them leave Egypt! How many times as a believer have you come to some experience in your life and said, "This is horrible. I never had anything like this as an unbeliever. Why, before I was a Christian everything went smoothly." That is exactly what the Jews said. Remember, this is the second generation of those that left Egypt who said, "this is no place of seed or figs, or of vines, or of pomegranates." Do you know what they are describing? Egypt! And they are saying, as believers who have been delivered from the bondage of Egypt, "Oh, that we were back in Egypt." But they are not thinking of the chains. They are not thinking of the lash of the taskmasters. They are thinking of the pleasant things. I have heard believers say, "Back in the world there were so many nice pleasant things, the people were always so sweet and treated me so kindly. Why, my unbelieving friends have been kinder to me than Christians." They long for the leeks and the garlic and the onions, and think only, as it says here, of the figs and the vines and the pomegranates. Every time you get in pressure, do you want to go back to something you had before? It is a very dangerous thing for a Christian who gets into pressure to look back—to look back into his previous life, back into the world, into the so-called pleasures in the world, the life of the world, from which he has been delivered. There are many believers who not only look back, but they are willing to turn back for something they desire. They are willing not to be identified with believers any more. But they can never change their identification with Christ.

Here was a generation who had arisen who, instead of trusting the Lord, fell into the same pattern as their fathers. They longed to return to Egypt. They wanted to go back into the world. Now this was a psychological sublimation. They wanted to substitute Egypt for the place of testing. It is human nature to want to get away from an unpleasant situation. When someone is in misery notice how people avoid them. Watch how friends stay away. They want to be around those who are gay and happy and flitting through life in a pleasant manner. But as soon as someone becomes a little sad or depressed, there is a wide detour around that person. These Israelites now think of Egypt as being a gay, pleasant, happy place. Oh, to go back to Egypt. Oh, the fun we could have in Egypt. There is plenty of water there. Why, there is the Nile river, just full of water. In reality they have failed the test because they did not do the very first thing that all of us should do in our "no water" situation. "In everything give thanks: for this is the will of God in Christ Jesus concerning you" (I Thessalonians 5:18).

Let me ask you a frank question, but give your answer to God. Have you thanked the Lord for that "no water" problem you have in your life? Everyone has some problem—have you thanked the Lord for yours? Do you thank Him every day for it? Do you wake up and say, "Father, this is Thy day. I am still breathing and I am still alive because of thy grace. What do you have for me today? And thank you, Father, for the terrible adversity that I have." Then, are you aware that "all things work together for good" (Romans 8:28)? Do you recognize that you cannot grow into the mature believer God wants you to be spiritually and that you cannot count for Him until your faith is tested?

When you attend a football game, do you think those boys run out on the field because they happen to be a little bigger than anyone else? I should say not. That does not mean a thing. There are hours and hours of push-ups, duck waddles, running, stopping, starting, falling, hitting, charging and all the rest of it, for hours and hours and hours. This is the testing period. Finally they get to run out on the field and either play or sit on the bench, because they have worked for hours and hours and hours! They have been tested, tested, tested! They started in August when you were looking for shade somewhere, and they almost died the first few days. They would limp over to the side, they would become ill, then they would fall back in. They would run and run and run, weighted down with heavy padding and heavy uniform. It is the most agonizing training in the world. During the first few days of football practice there is scarcely a man who doesn't ask, "Is it worth it?" But if you survive the first few days, your mental attitude gradually changes. You develop coordination and muscular ability which enables you to go out on the field and play in such a manner that thousands of people cheer you.

In the secret place of practice, where no one else can see it, you are being constantly tested. We live in the generation where God has to cut 98 per cent of the squad because we cannot survive the "no water" test. I think that this is the weakest generation of believers that has ever lived: one, because we know so little doctrine; and two, we have claimed so few of the promises in the Word. We have not cracked the faith barrier. We have not moved into the life which God has provided for us. We spend time looking back toward Egypt, or looking at leadership, criticizing and complaining and blaming someone else. It doesn't have to. be Moses; it can be anyone who is near. We look for "scape-goats" on the one hand, and look back toward Egypt on the other.

*Verse 6.* Now notice the contrast in the attitude of Moses and Aaron: "And Moses and Aaron went from the presence of the assembly unto the door of the tabernacle of the congregation, and they fell upon their faces: and the glory of the Lord appeared unto them." They went to the door of the Tabernacle, inside the outer court, though they could have gone in. They had a right to, because they were both of the Tribe of Levi, both priests. There in this crisis they sought the Lord.

*Verses 7 and 8.* "And the Lord spake unto Moses, saying, Take the rod. . . ." This is a different rod from that with which he smote the river in Egypt, because there is a new analogy here. This is actually Aaron's rod that budded. "Take the rod, and gather thou the assembly together, thou and Aaron thy brother, and speak ye unto the rock. . . ." This is a different Hebrew word for rock from that found in Exodus 17:6. This word means an elevated rock, and it is a picture of Christ in resurrection. And you will notice, he is to *hold* the rod and *speak* to the rock. Just as Christ is smitten once for sin, now we speak to the resurrected Christ. There is a tremendous type here. So, He said,

"Speak ye unto the rock before their eyes; and it shall give forth his water, and thou shalt bring forth to them water out of the rock: so thou shalt give the congregation and their beasts drink." Of course, the analogy is the faith-rest life, for this time the water is blessing and strength. Now notice what follows, for this is the occasion which kept Moses from leading the people across Jordan and entering into Canaan. This is why Joshua was chosen to replace Moses.

*Verses 9 and 10.* "And Moses took the rod from before the Lord, as he commanded him. (So far, partial obedience). And Moses and Aaron gathered the congregation together before the rock, and he said unto them (now notice, this was NOT part of the instructions from the Lord), Hear now, ye rebels; must WE fetch you water out of this rock?" God in His grace saw fit to rebuke Israel not by words, but by action. But Moses could not resist the temptation to rebuke them verbally. He is going to make a speech which would have been all right, had God authorized it. There were times when He called them stiff-necked rebels, but not here. This time God had something to teach them about grace. However, He is forced to teach a lesson in grace even stronger than ever. He is going to be gracious with Moses. "Hear now, ye rebels, must we fetch you water out of this rock?" The "we," of course, is Moses and Aaron. Now Moses and Aaron cannot fetch water out of a rock. But Moses has had enough. He is fed up. He is tired of all of this—tired of the "Meribahing."

*Verse 11.* "And Moses lifted up his hand, and with his rod he SMOTE THE ROCK TWICE," contrary to divine instruction. In the face of such disobedience it is natural to think, "God will never bring water." But God is gracious, and in spite of Moses, out comes the water, and the type is preserved. Christ was smitten for us, once for the water of salvation. Now we speak to the Rock for the water of blessing. We speak to the resurrected Rock. And, notice the adverb used by the Spirit, "water came out *abundantly,* and the congregation drank, and their beasts also."

*Verse 12.* Then the Lord took Moses aside and put him in the woodshed. But He did it privately. You see, Moses was in the place of leadership, and it was to the Lord he must answer, not the congregation. "And the Lord spake unto Moses and Aaron, Because ye believed me not. . . ." Moses and Aaron are saved. Their salvation is not in view here. They failed to enter into faith-rest at this moment. They failed to crack the faith-barrier on this occasion.

"Because ye believed me not, to sanctify me (set me apart) in the eyes of the children of Israel, therefore ye shall not bring this congregation into the land which I have given them."

*Verse 13.* "This is the water of Meribah." Remember the Meribah! Remember the warning of unbelief, of failure to crack the faith barrier!

# THE NEW TESTAMENT APPLICATION OF MERIBAH
## HEBREWS 3:7-11

Hebrews 3:7-11 is a quotation of Psalm 95:8-11. "Harden not your heart, as in the provocation" (Psalm 95:8). "Provocation" is an old English word meaning the same as "chide" (Exodus 17: 2), or "chode" (Numbers 20:3), translated thus from the Hebrew word "Meribah." The Hebrew says literally, "Harden not your heart as in the Meribah, as in the day of testing in the wilderness."

Now look at it in Hebrews 3:7: "Wherefore as the Holy Spirit saith, Today (a continuous today; as pertinent now as it was then) if he will hear his voice. . . ." What is His voice today? The promises of the Word of God!

Will you hear His voice when He says:
> Fear thou not; for I am with thee: be not dismayed; for I am thy God: I will strengthen thee; yea, I will help thee; yea, I will uphold thee with the right hand of my righteousness (Isa. 41:10).

Will you hear His voice when He says:
> Casting all your care upon him, for he careth for you (I Peter. 5:7).

Will you hear His voice when He says:
> Cast thy burden upon the Lord, and he shall sustain thee: he shall never suffer the righteous to be moved (Psalm 55:22).

Will you hear His voice when He says:
> Trust in the Lord with all thine heart; and lean not unto thine own understanding. In all thy ways acknowledge him, and he shall direct thy paths (Prov. 3:5, 6).

Will you hear His voice when He says:
>    Delight thyself also in the Lord; and
> he shall give thee the desires of thine heart.
> Comit thy way unto the Lord; trust also in him;
> and he shall bring it to pass (Psalm 37:4, 5).

Oh, when are we going to learn to crack the faith barrier, to move into this place of the moment-by-moment Sabbath? Into this place of perfect peace?

*Verse 8.* "If you will hear his voice (the Word of God; the promises), Harden not (through habitual unbelief and refusal to trust) your hearts (that is, your mind; the part of the frontal lobe which exercises faith or unbelief), as in the provocation (MERI-BAH), in the day of testing in the wilderness." What is the third chapter of Hebrews saying to us today? In the past God had a moment-by-moment Sabbath for His people. He gave them promises. He demonstrated His faithfulness, and then He put them in the place of testing, and said, "Will you trust Me, or won't you?" And they failed! Now, God says to you today, "are you going to fall into the pattern of failure, or are you going to trust Me? You have trusted Me for the big thing, salvation; will you trust Me for the needs of your life—that "no water" situation that you face right now? Will you trust Me for that?" Will you hear His warning, "Harden NOT your hearts as in the day of provocation, in the day of testing in the wilderness, when your fathers tested me, proved me, and saw my works forty years?" He was faithful to them for forty years.

*Verse 10.* "Wherefore I was grieved with that generation, and said, They do alway err (wander) in their heart; and they have not known my ways." Notice, ignorance of His ways. Not only did they fail to trust Him, to mix the promises of God with faith, but the Holy Spirit says here, "They don't even KNOW about my moment-by-moment Sabbath, even though it is there, even though it exists." Here is something that belonged to them, and they did not claim it. Here is something that belongs to you today, as a believer. Have you claimed it?

*Verse 11.* "So I sware (the solemn, divine oath) in my wrath (an expression of divine discipline), They shall not enter into my rest." And, as God promised, most of that generation did not, the only exceptions being Caleb and Joshua.

*Verse 12.* "Take heed, brethren (believers today), lest there be in any of you an evil heart of unbelief (it is evil to refuse to believe the promises of God), in departing from the living God (literally, 'keep standing off from the living God')." It is possible for people to be eternally saved, to possess eternal salvation, but to stand off from God in time. If you are facing a "no water" situation today, if you are falling apart, if you are upset, if you are disturbed, what is the matter? You are standing off from God who is waiting to bless you. But He will not bless you until you crack the faith barrier. "Stand still, and watch the deliverance of the Lord" (Exodus 14:13). "They that wait upon the Lord shall 'exchange their strength for His'" (Isaiah 40:31). "To wait" means to keep trusting, to trust moment by moment. "They that wait upon the Lord shall renew their strength (exchange their strength for His); they shall mount up with wings as eagles; they shall run and not be weary; and they shall walk, and not faint."

What is the strength of the Christian life? It is in standing still. It is in God's gracious provision of the moment-by-moment Sabbath, which is now called "rest." The word "rest" is used synonymously with "Sabbath," for the Hebrew word "Sabbath" means rest. Every phase of Christian experience, including rebound (I John 1:9), and prayer, depends on understanding and using the faith-rest technique.

*Verses 13-15.* "But exhort (encourage) one another daily, while it is called Today; lest any of you be hardened through the deceitfulness of sin (refusing to believe the Word). For we are made partners with Christ, if we hold the beginning of our confidence stedfast unto the end; (In other words, if we keep trusting Him, if we mix the promises of God with faith to the end of our troubles or our "no water" situation); While it is said, Today, if ye will hear His voice, harden not your hearts, as in the Meribah."

Right now most of us face a "no water" situation—a hopeless situation of some kind or another, and it seems at this moment the most difficult thing in the world. Those of you with a heavy heart may be thinking, "I don't know if I can stand it much longer; I don't know if I can take it." But when God puts you in the furnace of fire, the furnace of suffering, He wants you to do only one thing—trust Him! Believe His Word! Mix the promises of God with faith! Move into this place of perfect peace, perfect rest and perfect confidence. That is what Peter meant when he said in I Peter 1:7, "That the trial of your faith, being much more precious than of gold that perisheth, though it be tried with fire (great crisis), might be found unto praise and honor and glory at the appearing of Jesus Christ."

"Though it be tried by fire," a "no water" situation. As a believer in Jesus Christ, you have your greatest opportunity right now, for the darker the outlook, the more difficult the adversity, the greater the problem, the more He is glorified when we crack the faith barrier, when we can keep on trusting Him. "For without faith, it is impossible to please him" (Hebrews 11:6a). Remember the Meribah!

# THE DEFINITION OF THE FAITH-REST LIFE

## HEBREWS 4:1

We might title Hebrews 4, "How to be happy though a Christian." Perhaps you are thinking this is in jest, but it is not. Do you realize that the most difficult state for a Christian to achieve is happiness? Are you aware that the pressures against the believer in Jesus Christ are a thousand-fold greater than that of the unbeliever? This does not sound exactly like a sales talk for Christianity, and this would hardly be the place to give an invitation to accept Christ as Saviour. But I think as believers we ought to face the facts. It is harder to be happy in this world as a Christian than for an unbeliever to be happy. It is much easier for an unbeliever to be happy, temporarily, of course, and sometimes for a very short period, simply because he is free from the tremendous, powerful, insidious pressures that are brought to bear on the believer in Jesus Christ. Often the greater the capacity for service and the greater the believer can be used, the greater are the pressures against him from all sides—the world, the flesh and the devil. As you know, the Air Force has cracked the sound barrier. But overcoming one obstacle has created others. Somewhere between twice and three times the speed of sound there is a tremendous heat problem. We now have to find a way to keep a pilot cool at a temperature of 500 or more degrees. Yet the difficulties of cracking the sound barrier are nothing compared to cracking the faith-rest barrier, that is, the moment-by-moment Sabbath barrier.

A Navy pilot, with whom I recently had an interesting discussion, related a most amazing experience. While flying a jet, he shot *himself* down. Going into a shallow dive, he fired his gun through the jet squeeze, then steepened his dive so that his speed increased beyond the velocity of the shells he had fired. He not only passed them, but as he began to pull out of the dive, he pulled up into his shells, which hit his plane and knocked him out of the sky. This illustrates very graphically what we have done with speed. We can fire bullets, pass them, catch up with them and be shot down by them!

That is nothing compared with what we do to ourselves when we fail to crack this faith-rest barrier! We miss the wonderful and beautiful valley of blessing just over a ridge called faith. The trouble is, the ridge does not look as though there would be any green pastures on the other side. As a result, we who believe in Jesus Christ begin to deviate into all sorts of ideas and activities, missing the perfect place God has for every believer. Just as God has graciously provided salvation for us for all eternity; just as we KNOW our sins are forgiven and blotted out and that we are cleansed from all iniquity; just as we can KNOW that we have the righteousness of God imputed to us and that we possess eternal life, that we are now His children and the objects of His infinite, marvelous, matchless love; just as we can KNOW right now that God has a purpose for us by keeping us here by the very fact that we are alive and breathing today, means that God has something for us today, tomorrow and the next day. And just as we recognize the reality of our salvation, the reality of our temporal existence, we need to recognize that God has not forgotten our special need of happiness, of peace, of joy, of strength. God not only had us in mind when Jesus Christ took our place and went to the cross and died for our sins, but God had us in mind when He provided this wonderful moment-by-moment Sabbath. All God is asking us to do is to walk over the next ridge by a step of faith.

We came to a ridge called Calvary, and there we accepted Jesus Christ as Lord and Saviour. We approached that cross by faith. We received Jesus Christ, we trusted in Him, we accepted the condition that "Whosoever believeth in Him shall not perish, but have everlasting life" (John 3:16). Now God enjoins us to move over the next ridge. If you don't, the world, the flesh and the devil, with their power and their pressures, with their strategy will, together, neutralize your testimony. We need to realize that as believers we are vulnerable, that we can become upset and depressed, that we can be destroyed by the activities of our own human nature, our own sin nature, unless we move over this next ridge. Thus in verse 1 of chapter 4 we have the exhortation or warning of failing to reach the goal of the faith-rest life.

Verse 1. "Let us (believers) therefore (in view of the experiences of the Jews in chapter 3) fear. . . ." Generally speaking, believers are commanded not to fear in the Christian way of life (II Timothy 1:7). Here is the exception. We are to be afraid of not entering into the faith-rest life. Without the faith-rest technique we cannot have the perfect happiness and blessing which belongs to every believer in time.

"Let us therefore fear, lest a promise being left us of entering into his rest, any of you should seem to come short of it." The promises—those in God's Word dealing with time rather than eternity—are in danger of being left unclaimed. The promises are left behind in writing, and are continually waiting for believers to claim them. By claiming God's promises we enter into temporal rest. This is the definition of the faith-rest life. We crack the faith barrier. We move over the ridge.

## THE MECHANICS OF THE FAITH-REST TECHNIQUE
### HEBREWS 4:2, 3

Verse 2. "For unto us was the gospel preached, as well as unto them: but the word preached did not profit them, not being mixed with faith in them that heard it." A contrast is set up between the Exodus generation of believers and believers today. The analogy is obvious. They had promises; we have promises. They failed to claim the promises; we must not follow their example. The promises of the Word are only profitable when they are mixed with our faith. This involves two principles: *knowing* the promises and *believing* them. The promises can be learned by study and memorization, but they can only be appropriated by faith. Seven thousand sacks of cement in a warehouse are actually no good until they become concrete. To become concrete they must be mixed with water and sand in the right proportions. Before the promises of God for time become concrete, they must be mixed with our faith. There is no substitute for claiming the promises of God.

*Verse 3.* "For we who have believed do enter into rest, as he said, As I have sworn in my wrath, if they shall enter into my rest: although the works were finished from the foundation of the world."

God is still saying to us today, "If you have trusted in Christ, if you have received Him as your Lord and Saviour, I have many wonderful things for you, but you must stand still to receive them." If we, as believers, would just stand still for a minute, He could give us something, He could provide something. But we cannot seem to stand still. We have to be on the go. We have to be doing something, thinking up something. We are seeking this elusive thing called happiness. We are trying to find something that will give some stimulation, satisfaction, peace or blessing to self. And the more we move, the harder it is for God to provide this for us. He says, "Stand still so that I can bless you." If we would first stand still to receive what God has provided, then we could really move, and in the right direction and at the right time. Here it is called rest—God's gracious, matchless, endless provision for believers in time. The word "rest" is the same Hebrew word as "Sabbath," and it is a moment-by-moment Sabbath. There is only one way to get into this place, and that is by FAITH.

"We which have believed." "We" refers to every believer; "believed"—not at any particular time, or at any specified occasion —but "believed" the promises after salvation. Notice, it does not say "we which have worked up an emotional reaction or an emotional experience, or we who have rationalized, or thought our way through, or we who have worked our way through." "We who have BELIEVED do enter into his rest." It all goes back to the appropriation of grace in the only manner possible—by faith!

Another facet of this valley of rest is that it is located anywhere. It is located in Berachah Church. It is located in any part of Houston, in any part of Texas or in any part of the world. There is a moment-by-moment Sabbath which God has provided for us, but we have to walk over the ridge of faith to move into it—wherever we are.

Now, you remember that in order to enter into this rest we must get hold of the promises of the Word, and we must claim them by faith. And we, as believers, can enter at any moment we will believe the Word. But notice, God has said back in chapter 3, "So we see they could not enter in because of UNBELIEF." Referring back to that group of believers in the Old Testament, those in the wilderness who refused to trust God, here is an astounding fact. I have read and re-read the history of those believers. For forty years God provided everything. He provided the picture of their salvation—their deliverance from Egypt. He provided the way through the Red Sea. He provided the blood of the atoning lamb. He provided guidance for them by day. He provided navigational aids by night in the pillar of fire. He provided a perfect textbook for them concerning the Person and work of Jesus Christ through the Tabernacle, the holy days and the Levitical offerings. He not only provided these great spiritual benefits, but at the same time He provided a seventh day for them. They were to rest. They were to do nothing. They were to be occupied with the Lord. This was to remind them of what He had provided for them every moment. He provided shoes for their feet. He provided clothing, knowledge in time of war, deliverance from their enemies, their problems and their difficulties. For forty years God was faithful day after day. But day after day after day they turned against Him. They complained. They were bitter. They longed for the leeks and garlic and onions and the pomegranates—all the nice things they remembered from Egypt. They forgot His faithfulness, they forgot His provision and they chose to ignore it. As a result, we see forty years of misery. They were believers, yet those people were continually miserable because they would not enter into a moment-by-moment Sabbath. They would not trust Him. They would not lean on Him. Nor was their misery the only tragic result. There were hundreds of people, nations with whom they came in contact, who went to an eternal lake of fire because the Israelites had no testimony; they had no power. Everything in the Christian life, everything in the believer's experience by way of power and strength and ability and testimony comes from rest. Without rest we have absolutely nothing in the spiritual life. Without this moment-by-moment Sabbath, without trusting Him, we are powerless!

I do not know what kind of a week you had, but if it has been a normal week, you have had heartbreaks, problems, difficulties and trials. Perhaps you have been depressed, disturbed, upset, or sitting on the "panic button." Many times as we look back over a past week we can see so much that would break our hearts; then we stop and think of just how wonderful the Lord really is. How gracious He is. From all these pressures and difficulties and heartaches and problems there are only two reactions as far as we as believers are concerned. Today we can stand at the threshold and choose one or the other. We can choose one little valley, the faith-rest life. We can choose the one place where we can enter into a moment-by-moment Sabbath. We can choose to believe the Word, or we can choose to be miserable, entirely and utterly miserable, until the day we depart from this earth. We can either believe the Word and enter into this perfect peace and rest, or we can hit the panic button and be miserable!

An unbeliever gets his happiness from dependence upon some person, some thing, some event, some position in life or some measure of success, but for the one who believes in Jesus Christ, God has provided perfect happiness through a place of rest, a place which does not depend upon any human factor in life. This place is a complete dependence upon the One who is the source of joy and strength, the Lord Jesus Christ. By dependence upon Him, we are able to help other believers as well as unbelievers. The secret of this whole passage is in one little word in verse 3, "rest."

Now God is so wonderful to us that it is impossible for us to fully realize it. God does some amazing things for us experientially to try to get us to move into this rest. Just as you would try to herd cattle into a special place in order to feed them, so God tries to herd us into this special place. He permits suffering; He permits trial; He permits us to run around and to bump our heads on this wall and that wall, until we get knots on our heads. He permits us to hit the "panic button." He permits us to get discouraged and upset. He permits us to go through all of these things so that we will wake up and realize there is no rest or peace or satisfaction until we move into this Sabbath which He has provided for us, this moment-by-moment rest.

After reading this passage many times, perhaps even more in the original Greek language than in the English, I realized one day that the key to understanding it was found back in chapter 3, verse 7, "Today if ye will hear his voice. . . ." I was missing the whole point of the passage. I wasn't listening. Now, how many times have you seen this passage and have not heard a thing? It's here, but we don't HEAR it! We do not hear this particular word "rest." Yet God has given it to us. This is for us. And that is why one of the most gracious things God does for us is to give us difficulties and hardships so that we will wake up and realize He wants us to be right in the center. In the center of the hurricane there is a spot where there is no storm, where it is calm and quiet. The trouble with us is that we are all around this central spot. We are in the hurricane being blown this way and that, upside down, feet over head and head over feet. We have no stability; yet God says, "Look—in the eye of the hurricane it is peaceful." In the midst of all of our troubles and difficulties God says, "Move into the center!" In the eye it is quiet. Just believe the Word. Claim the promises by faith. Move into this moment-by-moment Sabbath. It is the very center of His plan for us. He has already told us how. Mix the promises of God with faith!

So, He is saying in verse 3, Look! here is the decision for the "decider" of every believer to make, for every time there is any problem or any difficulty or any adverse situation, you face a crisis. You can try your own answer, you can go through all the motions and activities of psychological sublimation and compensation, but do you know why you are still here? Do you know why I am still here? To glorify Him, to glorify Christ! God says, "I want you, believer, to lean on Me, to trust Me. And to make it easy I have given you some crutches. I have given you the Word, the promises from the Bible, and I want you to claim them. First, I want you to know them, and then I want you to claim them." God wants you to have a moment-by-moment Sabbath. He wants you to be so stabilized that you can take anything that life has to offer, including one of the most difficult things—prosperity, or the approbation of man. Through a stabilized life, He wants us to be a blessing and a help to others, and to cause wonderful, precious souls to come to know Christ as their personal Lord and Saviour. He wants us to be living proof that Christ is the answer. But the whole life falls apart unless we move into this one spot called "rest."

"As He said, As I have sworn in my wrath. . . ." This is an anthropopathism by which God is expressing Himself in human terms to show an attitude—to show that He cannot pour out any blessing, nor supply any need unless we will trust Him. Unless we will wait for Him. Unless we will stand still and let Him pour it out. The word "if" is deceiving, because the structure of the Greek in this sentence gives the force of an emphatic negative assertion or oath. God is saying literally, "As I have sworn in my wrath, they shall *not* enter into my rest." Why didn't they enter into His rest? For one reason only, and that is found in the previous verse—they did not mix the promises of God with faith. They refused to believe the Word. Now God said to that generation, and He says to us today, "Won't you believe the Word? Won't you lean on Me? Won't you stop depending on yourself?"

One of the paradoxes in the Christian life is that so frequently God must make us completely miserable in order to make us completely happy. He often must remove every human and material crutch we lean upon before He can bless us. We think, "My answer to happiness is this . . . person," and we lean on that person. So God kicks that prop out from under us. Then we say, "It is this . . . thing." And God kicks that prop out from under us. We try this and we try that; we think this is necessary, and God removes them all. The time may come very shortly when God will kick all the props out from under us in this wonderful way of life we have in this country. There may be a time very shortly when you will long for the luxury of a good, hot bath. God is trying to tell us, "There is only one thing that is necessary, and that is to trust Me, to lean on Me!" This is not believing for just a second or even a day, but trusting Him no matter how tough things get, no matter how long it takes. Wait on the Lord! Believe Him! Every time we turn on our "decider" and say, "I believe," then God is glorified, the Son is pleased with us and our lives are changed. Otherwise, we as Christians are the sorriest people in the world. Of course, that may not be true of you, but it certainly is true of me. I know of no worse person in the world than myself when I am out of fellowship. Now, don't all of you nod your heads that way ! It is true with all of us.

God did not intend for us to live out of fellowship. That is why He made provision for us to be restored to fellowship (I John 1:9) and thereby to be controlled by God the Holy Spirit. He also made provision for us to stabilize and to move. He did not say we had to have materialistic things, or that we had to have a relationship, or a person, or an event or the approbation of men. God says, "You have to have Me!" Colossians 2:10, "Ye are complete in Him." It becomes necessary sometimes for God to take everything away from us in order to understand that. He may have to make us so miserable that we will crawl in the dust. God does not want to do that, but He may have to so that we will learn to trust Him, to lean on Him, to delight in Him. "Delight thyself also in the Lord and he shall give thee the desires of thine heart. Commit thy way unto the Lord; Trust also in him, and he shall bring it to pass" (Psalm 37:4, 5). The word "trust" actually says, "keep trusting also in him." But you know how we trust Him, don't you? "Oh Father, I'm in an awful situation. I'm as miserable as I can be. I know I Peter 5:7 is there, and so here it is, Lord, I'm committing my problems to you. I am trusting you." "The battle is the Lord's." "This is your problem, Father; You take it and work it out." Then . . . "I just thought of something, Lord. Give it back—I'm going to try this first." So I try something, and it falls all apart. Then becoming miserable again, I turn it back over to the Lord, and for a few minutes I have perfect peace. But all of a sudden, a thought—and I say, "Just thought of an answer! Give it back!" And so we spend most of our time passing our problems back and forth, back and forth, while chewing our nails and churning inside.

This is exactly why we have the word "wait" in the Bible. Wait always means faith, but it is not trusting for a second, or for five minutes, it means KEEP trusting, KEEP trusting, as it says of Abraham, "He staggered not at the promise of God through unbelief; but was strong in faith, giving glory to God" (Romans 4:20). What does it mean to be "strong in faith?" He kept on trusting; he never stopped trusting, though all hope was gone. The whole angelic world above us, all those angels who have chosen for God, began to rejoice, for here was a member of the human race who could be kicked and kicked some more, yet all he did was to say, "Thank you, Lord, for the kick." He kept right on rolling until suddenly God said "That is enough!" Abraham, through faith, became one of the greatest saints who ever lived.

Along came another man. His name was Elijah. God gave Elijah a job to do. When Elijah finished he stood back and said, "All right now, Lord, pin on the medal." But the Lord said, "Oh no, I want you to go down to a creek and watch it dry up." Elijah complained, "This isn't fair, Lord." But the Lord sent Elijah into a far country to the home of a widow—not a wealthy widow—but a poor widow, and a Gentile at that! Elijah was a Jew. The Lord told Elijah that this poor widow would take care of him. God took a woman, a widow who was helpless, without food and in a desperate situation, who was on the verge of suicide, and used her to make Elijah a great man. Elijah learned to trust the Lord through a Gentile woman! After two years, God said, "All right, Elijah, you are ready to go back." Now God didn't take Elijah into the great courts of the nations round about. He didn't leave him in the land of Israel. He did not take him down into the temple in Jerusalem. He took him outside to a helpless person, and that helpless person taught Elijah the power of helplessness! Then Elijah went back into the land and led in the great revival.

God chose a young boy to be king of Israel who had learned the secret of waiting through tending a flock of sheep. David waited and waited. He watched those all around him advance, he saw them promoted and showered with favors, but he stood still and waited—waited until God said, "Move." Then God promoted him. But immediately David began to get kicked around again, and began to go through the most severe testings of his life. He had to learn to wait and wait some more, to learn to trust the Lord implicitly. Then it was that he moved into that realm of perfect peace and power and strength. But God had to train him through trial and difficulty.

Now notice the last phrase in *Verse 3:* ". . . although the works were finished from the foundation of the world." When God, the Lord Jesus Christ, created the world (Col. 1:16), at the same time He created everything to make the Christian happy. Did you hear that? Along with that which can be seen in the world, and that which cannot be seen, along with all of the theory of mass and energy (with apologies to Dr. Einstein) which exist in this creation, God also made special provision at creation for every person who would ever trust in Jesus Christ. He created a valley, a true "Fountain of Youth," but it is not located in Florida or in any particular geographical location, and Ponce de Leon never found it. He created something on the inside of every believer and provided something on the outside, the linking together of which makes for perfect peace and perfect happiness. It is faith on the inside and a promise from the Word on the outside! This passage is telling us that He has provided for us from the foundation of the world. And, if He provided it then, it is still in existence, as this passage will develop.

I wonder what per cent of Christians go through life and go home to be with the Lord never having found out what this Christian life is all about—never having discovered the moment-by-moment Sabbath, the place of rest and peace and joy which results in power and strength. Now I want you to be able to understand the pattern of your life today, that regardless of the initial cause of your problems, difficulties or trials, God is speaking to you through the Word and through those experiences. Though your heart may be broken, your problems difficult, the situation hopeless, He bids you to try the one thing that works—the only thing that works: continuous, unceasing trust! Wait on the Lord!

## THE HISTORY OF THE FAITH-REST LIFE

### HEBREWS 4:4-9

*Hebrews 4:4.* "For he spake in a certain place (Genesis 2:2, 3) of the seventh day on this wise. . . ." The seventh day, which is Saturday, is an illustration of this moment-by-moment rest, or Sabbath. He is going to use the seventh day as an illustration, for He says regarding the seventh day, "And God did rest the seventh day from all his works." That is, all of the work of creation. Immediately we ask the question, "Why did He rest?" Was God tired? Think of creating all of these galaxies, billions of light years away, literally millions and millions of celestial bodies which are a thousand times larger than this planet earth! Think of the tremendous traffic pattern involved with the millions of celestial bodies all moving at high rates of speed. Think of just the structure of this earth and of the most minute things on this earth, of the atom with its protons and electrons, and the amazing structure there. Think of that which we see that is solid; and yet, there is actually more space than solid. Think of the tremendous amount of work that went into that! And you say, "Well, no wonder He rested on the seventh day. I would be worn out too." But that is not the reason for His rest. He was not tired at all for He is God. He rested on the seventh day because there was nothing else to do! That is why the Jews were told to sit down on Saturday and do nothing, for it was a memorial that God had provided everything. They were told to stop sowing and planting and reaping every seventh year and let God provide food from heaven. Why? To remind them that everything was already provided. It is just as though I said to you, "Dinner is served," and although you were very hungry, you would turn your back and say, "No, thank you. I am not interested in food." God says to you today, "Dinner is ready and on the table. I have prepared for you in the presence of your enemies a table" (literally, Psalm 23:5). Your enemies are the world, the flesh and the devil. And He has prepared a ten-course dinner for you, starving believer, in the presence of your enemies. The table of food is waiting to be eaten—by faith. Believe the Word! Believe the promises! Claim the Word, apply the Word by faith, and then you will enter into what God has for you. That is why it says in Verse 4, "For he spake in a certain place of the seventh day on this wise, and God did rest the seventh day from all his works."

Let us go back to the original situation in the Garden of Eden. Suppose Adam, looking about in his orchard which God provided, not Adam, sees within inches of his head a big, luscious, juicy red apple, and he says, "Oh, I wish I had an apple; I'm so hungry for an apple, I can taste it. Oh, how I want that apple." Now this apple is right before his nose. What does Adam have to do? It is there; God provided it. Adam didn't work for it, nor fight for it. Neither did he deserve it. All he had to do was to take it. Now listen, the faith-rest life is here, right now! Faith reaches into it. Faith moves in and takes it. Oh, how we need to crack the faith barrier, and move into that place of peace.

Just as God provided everything physical and material for man, He also provided everything spiritual. It has its beginning at Calvary's cross where Jesus Christ died for our sins and took our place. We must come to the cross and claim its cleansing blood by faith in Jesus Christ. But too many stop there instead of moving on and claiming the promises He has for us, instead of trusting Him completely. We have already trusted completely for salvation, why can't we trust Him completely for everything else?

There is a beautiful suspension bridge across Niagara Falls. The story of how it was built illustrates our point perfectly. One day an engineer flew a kite across the falls—not just for fun, for he had a purpose. When it came down on the other side, he had it anchored so that there was a slender cord stretched across one side of the falls to the other. Now who would ever have dreamed that little cord would become a great suspension bridge? However, if he had stopped there, it would not have been anything. Many Christians stop right there, with a little cord across the falls. But he tied a heavier cord to the little cord and pulled it across, then a heavier cord and another and another, until soon there was a steel cable across those falls. To this was added another and another, and finally there was a powerful bridge there where people can cross and look down over the falls.

Spiritually we all start with a slender cord of faith, which is salvation. Now we need to pull the heavier ones across, then heavier ones and heavier ones, adding strength day by day to our Christian life. That is the faith-rest life, the continual moment by moment day by day trusting in Him. If I trusted Jesus Christ for my salvation, if I trusted Him for the greatest thing He could ever provide for me, if I trusted Him for eternal life and the forgiveness of all sins, if I trusted Him for the biggest thing, can I not trust Him for the little things—the problems, the difficulties? Can I lean on Him and ONLY on Him? Can I wait patiently for Him? Can I claim His Word? That is the issue today!

*The failure of the Exodus generation. Verses 5 and 6.* ". . . If they shall enter into my rest (speaking of the Jews in the wilderness). Seeing therefore it remaineth that some must enter therein, and they to whom it was first preached entered not in because of unbelief." "It remaineth" means to leave behind, to remain over. This faith-rest life remains over from the past, but only two of the Exodus generation entered in, Caleb and Joshua. But before there can be a decision to enter in or not to enter in, it must first be preached. The majority of the wilderness generation failed to believe the temporal promises of God, and thus did not enter into His rest.

*Verse 7.* Since the Exodus generation failed, what effect did it have on future generations? We find in David's day the rest was still open. "Again, he limiteth (or, literally, he marks out) a certain day, saying in David (that is, saying in the Psalms), Today, after so long a time; as it is said; Today if ye will hear his voice, harden not your hearts." Then we have the quotation from Psalm 95:7, 8. The writer says: "Today, after so long a time. . . ." In other words, even though they had failed in the day of the Exodus, the faith-rest life was still open in David's day. "Today if ye will hear his voice, harden not your hearts." As in the former generation, so the invitation remained open in David's day. If they would just believe the promises and the doctrines of God's Word, they could enter into this same rest.

*Verse 8.* The Jews also failed in Joshua's generation. "For if Jesus (literally, Joshua, the son of Nun, not the Lord Jesus Christ) had given them rest. . . ." (the generation which existed after the Exodus). "If" introduces a Greek second-class condition meaning "and he didn't." "If Joshua had given them rest, then would he not afterward have spoken of another day." Joshua's generation also failed to enter into the rest, they failed to completely conquer the land, they failed to enter in by claiming the promises, the doctrines and the other things which were given to them. They did not claim God's Word; they did not believe it; they did not enter into rest; and therefore that generation stood as a defeated generation as well.

*Verse 9.* Yet in spite of the failures of various generations in the past in which the faith-rest technique was definitely not used, even though believers were upset and disturbed and falling apart, it continues to exist. "There remaineth therefore a rest to the people of God." The people of God are those who have received Jesus Christ as their Lord and Saviour. The people of God are those who have believed in Him, as the Scripture says, "Whosoever believeth in Him shall not perish but have everlasting life" (John 3:16). "Ye are the sons of God by faith in Christ Jesus" (Gal. 3:26). The people of God are those believers who have entered into eternal life by trusting in Christ, and therefore have moved into a relationship with God in time. Part of this relationship is the faith-rest life, mixing the promises of God with our faith, claiming the promises of His Word and having that peace of God "which passes all understanding." "There remaineth" is in the present tense in the Greek and thus there keeps on remaining a rest to the people of God. So the faith-rest life is perpetuated right down to this moment, and will be as long as time on earth continues. There will always exist a provision which means peace and rest, joy and happiness and blessing, simply by claiming the promises and the doctrines of God's Word. "For we which have BELIEVED do enter into rest."

## THE CHARACTERISTICS OF THE FAITH-REST LIFE
### HEBREWS 4:10-16

The brief history in verses 4 through 9 shows that the faith-rest technique started when man started. Among other things, God provided for man a rest, and while it was interrupted by sin, the rest continues to be perpetuated. Our faith starts at the cross where we obtain eternal rest; then from that point on we claim the promises of God's Word for the blessings, the by-products and the monopolies of the Christian way of life in time.

Now what are the characteristics of the faith-rest technique? How can it be described? What are some of the ways of recognizing it and some of the things which we have to face in connection with this particular technique? Verses 10 through 16 describe these characteristics.

(1) *The characteristic of faith.* This rest is characterized first of all by faith—a perpetual faith, a continuous faith, a faith which is often called by the Bible "patience." Patience does not imply that we are to sit down and tap our foot without saying anything. Patience in the Bible refers to continual trust, to keep on believing the promises of God. Some of you may have claimed some of these marvelous promises which belong to us. "Casting all your care upon him, for he careth for you" (I Peter 5:7). "The battle is the Lord's" (I Sam. 17:47). "Stand still and watch the deliverance of the Lord" (Exodus 14:13). If you keep on believing

these, if you keep on claiming these promises and mixing them with your faith, then you enter into this rest, and you stay there. If you haven't realized it, these are times of unrest. It is difficult to find a clear-thinking American any more. The only clear thinking being done today is by people who have some doctrine in the frontal lobe. The situation is not very promising. And yet in spite of all of this there is an area in which we can have absolute and perfect peace, a peace which will cause us to be ready for the crisis when it comes. In a crisis we need people who can orient in a hurry, people who do not fall apart and sit on the "panic button," and who do not have to run and check in with a psychiatrist or psychologist, or who seek some other form of sublimation. We will have to have people who can stand in the crisis and mix the promises of God with faith. People who know "that all things work together for good to them who love God, to them who are the called according to his purpose" (Rom. 8:28). People who can stand in the gap. They will be the ones who are using the faith-rest technique.

Who are the people in the past who have seen the issues and stood fast? Those who knew God's Word and believed it. And thus it will ever be. Those who can stand in the crisis hour, whose backbone is straight because it is built upon the doctrine of God's Word, whose thinking is clear because it is based upon Scripture and the divine viewpoint, who are not snow-balled by the double-talk of people in public life and by the various slants of the press—only these will be able to stand in the crisis. It is not too far off to say that the world, with its modern communication system, is going mad rapidly. And the only antidote to it is the divine viewpoint. And who can stand and declare the divine viewpoint? Those who live the faith-rest life. Those who continually claim God's promises. Those who have claimed doctrine and use it.

Verse 10. "For he that is entered into his rest, he also hath ceased from his own works, even as God did from his." Here is stated the first characteristic of the faith-rest technique—faith, and not works. When you enter into this rest you let God do the fighting, as it were. The battle is turned over to the Lord—the problems, the trials, the difficulties that you face—all are turned over to Him. "For he that is entered. . . ." Now who is entered? The one who has "ceased from his own works." You do not cease from the energy of the flesh until you enter the faith-rest life. Until you utilize the faith-rest technique, you operate on the energy of the flesh. To the person who has not entered into the faith-rest life, spirituality is a system of hustling, a system of programming, a system of giving and doing and calling and yak-yaking and the pumping of hands and smiles, and a lot of exterior, superficial hypocrisy. Then one day you learn that you can relax spiritually. You enter into the faith-rest life, where it is no longer a matter of the energy of the flesh, the phony front and the hypocrisy and the religiosity, but you become a relaxed and stabilized individual. Even though things around you are falling apart, you have God's Word, you claim it, and you have the strength that comes from it. As you study, the Holy Spirit teaches you the Word, with the result that you claim these things and enter into a place of perfect peace. When you utilize the faith-rest technique you no longer operate on the energy of the flesh. "He has ceased from his own 'brand' of works." "His own" means his peculiar and individual brand, whatever it is, and it may be anything. It might be fasting or even starving, giving up something or taking on something, doing more than one physically should, or hustling in some manner around a local church. But the beauty of the faith-rest life is the ability to derive strength from the peace that comes through simply trusting.

   (2) *The characteristic of diligence. Verse 11.* "Let us labour therefore to enter into that rest, lest any man fall after the same example of unbelief." The Greek word here translated "labour," should more accurately be rendered "diligent" or "eager." The writer is inviting all Christians to join him in diligence or eagerness (not in works) to enter the faith-rest life. It is just as if the writer has said, "I have entered this faith-rest life; I find it wonderful beyond description. Come on in, the water's fine." Another factor in this phrase is a mental attitude toward the faith-rest technique. The word diligence also implies a mental attitude. We should have a mental attitude of eagerness to enter into this rest. This should be the most important thing in the world to us. Ponce de Leon made a most eager and diligent search for the legendary fountain of youth in Florida, though he was unsuccessful. We have in this word the same idea of diligence. Suppose I told you that 100 feet behind Berachah Church, slightly under the surface of earth there is a miraculous spring, the water of which if

drunk will guarantee that you can revert to the age you desire. There would be a lot of people out digging if they were absolutely convinced that what I said was true. Then suppose I added that in order to go over there and dig you must have the correct mental attitude—that of diligence. "Let us be diligent and go seek this fountain that gives us the age we desire." I have no doubt that everyone would rush out. Because of the right mental attitude you don't mind digging, you don't mind getting your clothes soiled. You wouldn't care to do it under ordinary circumstances, but now you have a great objective in mind. This is the connotation of this Greek word. It means there is an objective, the faith-rest life. This objective is so wonderful that once you obtain it you will never want to leave it as long as you are in this life. It is the rest which has been mentioned so many times in context, one we should be diligent to enter because it is the place of perfect happiness, adjustment, peace and blessing. The verse continues, "lest any man should fall after the example of unbelief." Those in the past, of course, failed to enter simply because of unbelief. This is the third time that unbelief has been mentioned in connection with this rest.

(3) *The characteristic of knowing the Word of God.* This is one of the most important characteristics of the faith-rest life. To summarize thus far, it is characterized first of all by faith, and not works. No energy in the flesh is involved. Secondly, it is characterized by diligence, or by an eager mental attitude to get in and to stay in. Now, thirdly, it is characterized by the Word of God. We have spoken of it before as living in God's Word. There can be no faith-rest life apart from *knowing* God's Word. It is not a certain feeling you get, but it is having the Word as the object of your faith. Verse 12 brings into focus this very vital factor in the faith-rest technique.

*Verse 12.* "For the word of God is quick, and powerful, and sharper than any twoedged sword, piercing even to the dividing asunder of soul and spirit, and of the joints and marrow, and is a discerner of the thoughts and intents of the heart." We have already seen that in order to enter into the faith-rest life it must be by faith, and not works, even as salvation is by faith. But the faith of the faith-rest life is a persistent faith. Here is the "rest." As is always the case, "to believe" is a transitive verb. It must have a subject and an object. In salvation the subject of the transitive verb "to believe" is any member of the human race, while the object is the Lord Jesus Christ, who is the Saviour. For example, in Acts 16:31, "Believe on the Lord Jesus Christ, and thou shalt be saved." But when it comes to the faith-rest technique, the object of the verb "to believe" is the Word of God. The subject is the *believer* in the Lord Jesus Christ. We must actually believe the Word. But you cannot believe the Word until you know the Word and understand it in its various components. For example, we need to understand the Word from the position of history, or dispensations; we need to see it from the standpoint of doctrine, and from the standpoint of the promises. All of these things that are found in God's Word must become the objects of our faith. There are five things about God's Word in this verse.

First, the Word of God is "quick" or "alive," as you have heard me translate it many times, for that is exactly what the verb in the Greek means. "Alive" is a present participle, which means it is always alive, or living, and could be translated, "the Word of God is constantly alive," or "the Word of God is constantly living." If you want to know what life really is, you have to go to the Word of God. Today people go through the motions of living, but they are not really living at all. If you want to understand what true living really is, if you want to live in a true manner, and if you want to get the most out of life, then you must have as your source the Scripture. The Word of God is living. And it is also the secret to life here, as well as hereafter.

The second descriptive phrase for the Bible is the word "powerful." The Word of God is habitually living and powerful. Now there are many words for power. The noun which is used here is our Greek word "energy," or operational power. Even as the secret to life is found in God's Word, so the secret to dynamics or operational power is found right here. The Word of God is divine operational power in action. Therefore, we must believe the Word of God, appropriate the Scriptures, the promises, the doctrines, etc., in order to have divine operational energy transferred into the life.

The third characteristic of God's Word is that it is "sharper than any twoedged sword." The word picture here is very interesting. The sword used here is the Greek word "Machaira." A Machaira, though a very short sword, was one of the greatest inventions of the ancient world. In order to get across how unusual was this weapon of the ancient world, I must first describe the other swords already in existence. One kind of sword which was very impressive in the ancient world was called the Romphaia, a broad sword, usually five to six feet long with a large double handle, used first of all by the Thracians. It was not worn in a scabbard, but carried over the shoulder, or sometimes by two men. When the barbarians used this sword, they would have to rear back and get cocked, as it were, then come through with a mighty swing once to the right or left, which always left the user off balance and vulnerable to counter-attack. Those who could jump or duck did so, and while the Romphaia swordsman was off balance, they had their turn. Now the trouble with the Romphaia was that though it was a very impressive thing, it only had one sharp edge. When the Romans first advanced on the barbarians, carrying only short little Machaira swords, the barbarians with their great Romphaias looked down the hill at the advancing Romans coming up with these little short jobs, and sat back and had a great big laugh. But the Romans had the last laugh. You will see why in a minute.

Another sword in the ancient world was the Zephos, which featured a sharp point, and that is all. The edges were useless in fighting, and the only way you could do in the enemy with the Zephos was with some kind of a thrust. You had one shot at him straight forward, and if he rolled, bobbed, pitched, ducked or managed to get out of the way somehow, you are again left most vulnerable, and it's his turn. So the Zephos lacked a great deal.

Then there was the Akinakes. This sword, invented in Persia, was not much of a combat sword because it had a dull point, dull edges, and was more ornamental than useful. Its handle was usually studded with precious stones, and therein lay its value.

Finally, there was the Dolon, a sword which was hidden in some object as a disguise, such as a staff or a cane, and again it had only one sharp point. Now what is this verse saying here? Well, let's take a look. The Romphaia has but one sharp edge. The Bible does not consist of a point here and a point there, but every bit of the Scripture is valuable. The same applies to the Zephos with its little sharp point on the end of a blade, and thus is not an accurate picture of the Word of God. The ornate Akinakes was not used, for the Bible is not simply beautiful literature as it is often presented in college. Neither was the Dolon used, for the Bible is not hidden in its meaning. But the Bible is called here the Machaira because the Machaira was the most fantastic and most unusual weapon of the ancient world when it was invented. Now, granted, we do not think of the Machaira in terms of inter-continental ballistic missiles, but in that day it was just about as ingenious a thing as ever came along, the Romans being the first to use it.

First of all the Machaira was short, which meant that anyone could handle it. One did not have to be a physical giant, for it was light and maneuverable. The second thing about the Machaira was that it never left the user off balance or vulnerable. You could thrust, parry or slash to the left or right without having to regain your balance. The secret to the Machaira was that it not only had a very sharp point, but both edges were sharp also, a feature no one had ever thought of before. Some had one sharp edge or one sharp point, but no one ever thought of putting the whole thing together in one package. As a result the Roman soldiers cleaned up on the barbarians with this weapon. It was one of the most revolutionary inventions of the ancient world, and it is the weapon which is used in this verse. And what does it mean? It means simply that every jot and every tittle of God's Word is valuable and important. Every jot and tittle of God's Word is useable to us as Christians. The Christian who uses God's Word is never off balance. And there are many Christians who are off balance today. The Christian who uses God's Word is oriented and stabilized, which is one of the things that characterizes the faith-rest life. You cannot have the faith-rest life without God's Word, for this is the source of the promises and doctrines. The doctrine of "Divine Essence" alone can resolve every problem in life when applied to the situation. This is actually what the promises do. "Casting all your care upon him; for he careth for you," is simply an application of the doctrine of Divine Essence (Love) to the situation. "Jesus Christ, the same yesterday, today and forever" (Heb. 13: 8). Here is implied God's divine characteristic of faithfulness, or immutability. Applying immutability to the situation, He is always faithful, He never changes, He never lets us down. Thus various aspects of Divine Essence can be applied to a given situation in such a way that you come up with perfect stability.

The fourth characteristic of the Word in verse 12 is that the Bible penetrates, it pierces. It is not only a sword, it is a sword that cuts deep. Most of you at some time or another have been cut by the Word. Perhaps you did not realize it at the time, but you recognize that sooner or later the Bible is going to hit you hard. Let us put it this way, the Bible hits all of us, but hard! Piercing, in the present tense in the Greek, indicates that it keeps on piercing. It is also in the middle voice, whereby we understand here that when God's Word pierces or penetrates us it benefits us. This is the only time you can get whacked with a sword and be benefited by it. When God's Word penetrates, it benefits. The Word penetrates in the sense of going into the immaterial part, or the inner being, and lodging there, as indicated in the next phrase: "piercing even to the dividing asunder of the soul and the spirit." The Bible divides and separates the immaterial part of a man. The Bible is the only book that recognizes that the immaterial part of man, that is, regenerate man, has two parts. The Bible is the only book in the world that recognizes that man has more than a soul. Regenerate man also has an activated human spirit. And so the Bible continually penetrates into man, even to the immaterial part of man. Now you could stab someone with a knife or sword and penetrate the material part of man, his body. But suppose I handed you a sword and said, "Go out and stab a soul." You couldn't do it. Where is it? Where do you start? Would you stab the brain? or the throat? Where is the soul—in some part of the torso? We don't know where it is, but it is there! It is impossible for any sword, or bullet, or anything else to penetrate the immaterial part of man. That is what this word means. The Word of God pierces the soul and the spirit, and nothing else in the world can do it. Though you should literally riddle the body with machine gun bullets, you would never touch the soul. The soul cannot be penetrated by any weapon that has ever been invented. It can only be penetrated by God's Word, a force so powerful that it will even penetrate the immaterial part of man. Do you ever think about using it? Are there people who in some way disturb you, people who upset you, or someone who has it in for you? Use God's Word. It can change your attitude, it can change their's. It gets inside and changes the life. It goes in and gives peace and calm. It enters in and saves a soul, when all of our words, all of our arguments, all of our methods glance off as a bullet ricocheting against a stone wall. We never need to defend ourselves against those who would hurt us. Let the Word do it. We never need to defend the Word against those who defame it. The Word of God defends itself when you put it into action.

The illustration which is suggested by the next phrase is a medical analogy. ". . . piercing even to the dividing asunder of soul and spirit, even as the joints and the marrow. . . ." A surgeon in the medical profession, by his understanding of physiology, can take a knife or a surgical instrument and make a penetration successfully in order to heal, in order to help, and even as by the cutting he performs a successful operation, so the Bible performs a successful operation by getting inside of the soul and the spirit. The final characteristic of the Word goes on to develop how it does this.

The Bible is a "discerner of the thoughts and intents of the heart." 300 years ago a discerner was a judge. In that day someone who discerned a case between two people was as clearly understood as we understand the function of a judge today. The Greek word here means a judge, a critic, a critical judge, and that is what the Bible does for us. The Bible judges us daily and constantly, and we should be thankful for its judgment because it points the error of our ways so that we can rebound and get in fellowship and use the things that God has provided. And notice how the Bible judges. The Bible is a judge of thoughts. Some other member of the human race cannot judge your thoughts. Now you can do a pretty good job sometimes of guessing what people are thinking and be right on the button, for people often show what they are thinking. But no one can consistently tell what anyone else is thinking, and there are times when you couldn't even come close. But the Bible knows how and what you think and criticizes it and judges it. If you are envious of someone, if you are jealous, if you are proud, if you are vain, if your motives are false, the Bible judges them. The Bible is a judge or critic of "thoughts and intents." The word "intents" means motivation. Thus the Bible judges the thoughts and motivations of the heart, or the inner life, or the mind. In this way the operation is performed, the sin is cut out through confession (I John 1:9), and a life is restored.

(4) *The characteristic of divine inspection.* Even as the Bible can read our thoughts and our motives, we also have one above, God Himself, who reads our thoughts. How would you like to have everything you have thought today projected right above your head on the ceiling? Anybody want to take that test? Suppose I had a button here which when pushed, caused all your thoughts to appear on the ceiling above you. I would probably read it and quit! I cannot tell what you are thinking all the time and you cannot tell what I am thinking. But there is Someone who knows what we think every second, and this thinking becomes the basis of divine inspection.

*Verse 13.* "Neither is there any creature that is not manifest in his sight (in God's sight): but all things are naked and opened unto the eyes of him with whom we have to do." God knows what we are thinking all of the time. That is why God's Word is a judge of our thoughts, for in God's Word we have a good panorama of what we think, of what man in general thinks. And so here is set forth the principle that this rest involves continuous inspection of our thought pattern. Now, why our thoughts? Why the inner part of man? Because the faith-rest technique is not something we do on the outside, it is something we do in the mind. The faith-rest technique is on the inside, not on the outside. The faith-rest technique is not designed to make anyone into a professional bum or to give someone the excuse to stop working. The faith-rest technique is designed to give one perfect happiness at all times, in spite of circumstances, and to orient to every circumstance of life. The phrase "with whom we have to do" is literally, from the Greek, "with whom we have to give an account," or "to whom we have to give an account." The Lord Jesus Christ is going to take an account from us, and for this reason we are under constant examination.

(5) *The characteristic of witnessing.* This rest involves witnessing for Jesus Christ. Witnessing is the responsibility of every Christian, not just of pastors, assistant pastors, evangelists, Sunday School teachers and deacons. If you are a Christian, you are a witness for the Lord Jesus Christ, and if you live the faith-rest life you are going to walk into witnessing situations constantly. You will continually be presented with opportunities to speak a word, or more than a word, for the Lord Jesus Christ.

*Verse 14.* "Seeing then that we have (we keep on having) a great high priest (the Lord Jesus), that is passed into the heavens (perfect tense, He is passed in the past, with the result that He remains in heaven), Jesus the Son of God. . . ." And now here is the characteristic, "let us hold fast our profession," namely, witnessing. "Hold fast" means to cling tenaciously. It is in the present tense in the Greek, so "let us keep on clinging tenaciously, with all of our might to our profession," which is witnessing. The mood is subjunctive, by which the writer is inviting all of his readers to join him in witnessing for Jesus Christ.

(6) *The characteristic of testing.* This rest involves constant testing. Most of you know that muscles are built up by testing, and remain strong and useful by continual testing. The principle of weight lifting is a testing of muscles, which builds them up and makes them strong. It takes the weight in order to test them, in order to keep them in a constant state of power and strength. That is the way with the faith-rest life. It must be tested to become strong. And it is tested. Many of the problems and trials and adversities which come our way are designed to test us. Do we stay in the faith-rest life or not? Do we continue to trust the Lord? Do we continue to depend upon Him? Do we continue to claim the promises of God's Word? Do we rest in Him? Do we trust His Word? Do we claim His promises? That is why God continually permits testing in our life. So we have trials; we have problems that have no human solution. We have things which are beyond us, things which have no obvious way out. These test us to stay in the faith-rest life, to claim His promises, to live in His Word, to believe and to use the things which He has provided for us. Therefore, you can expect as long as you live periodic testing. And occasionally the roof will fall in or the rug will be pulled out from under you or your whole world will seemingly collapse, constituting even a greater test—a crisis test to see if you will still claim these promises and live in the Word. Sooner or later every Christian will face some kind of a crisis. And the big issue in that crisis is this: Do I believe God's Word? Will I claim God's Word or will I fall apart? Will I get upset? Will I be disturbed? Will I become disoriented in some manner? Will I live in "panic palace?" Or will I continue to claim those promises which are pertinent to the situation? "All things work together for good." "The battle is the

Lord's." "Stand still and watch the deliverance of the Lord." "Fear thou not for I am with thee." "For with God nothing shall be impossible." Will I claim these promises or not? Will I continue to live in the faith-rest life? So there must be testing.

*Verse 15.* "For we have not an high priest which cannot be touched with the feeling of our infirmities; but was in all points tested like as we are, yet apart from sin." We have not a high priest who did not go through these things. The Lord Jesus pioneered the way before us, and He was tested in every way that we are tested, yet never once did He sin. So the Lord Jesus Christ has traveled the road of testing. He has seen everything that can happen to us. He knows these things, and as I Corinthians 10:13 tells us, "he has provided a way of escape, that we may be able to bear it, or bear up under it."

(7) *The characteristic of prayer. Verse 16.* The phrase "let us" tells us we have come to the fourth and final hortatory subjunctive in this passage. Again, the hortatory subjunctive implies that the writer of the epistle is inviting his readers, all believers, to join him in something. He says, "let's all get together at the throne of grace." Join me in prayer. "Let us therefore come boldly unto the throne of grace." Something else we should note about this particular verb is the fact that it is in the middle voice. Here the middle voice means that the subject is benefited. Therefore prayer benefits the believer. We, as believers, are the subject and we are benefited by coming to God in prayer. The verb is in the present tense. We are to keep on coming constantly to the throne of grace. In other words this phrase actually says, "pray without ceasing," keep on praying, keep on coming to the throne of grace. So we have noted three things: the tense is present, it is something we should constantly do; the mood is subjunctive, hortatory subjunctive, we are to join the writer in prayer before the throne of grace; the voice is middle, we are benefited by prayer; and the meaning is to enter into the presence of the Lord through prayer. The word "boldly" means literally, "with boldness." We as believers, living the faith-rest life, can come boldly to the throne of grace, or with boldness. Now no one can enter into the presence of God with boldness. That is unthinkable! That is not possible! The very majesty of God would exclude such a thing. But we can come boldly by the use of the faith-rest technique. How does this work

out? Matthew 21:22, "All things whatsoever ye shall ask in prayer, believing, ye shall receive." And this word "with boldness" means to come with confidence. We can come with the utmost confidence to the throne of grace. We can say, "Father," we can offer a prayer and have confidence with regard to that prayer because we *believe*. We have mixed the promises of God with faith. You will notice that prayer is a throne of grace: we do not earn it, we do not deserve it, we do not have the right, humanly speaking, to come, but because of God's grace this is now possible. And then there is a purpose stated in this particular verse. It begins with the word "that," which introduces a purpose clause. "That we may obtain mercy. . . ." And again we have an aorist tense, in a point of time we may obtain mercy; subjunctive mood, which means the obtaining of this mercy is potential. It is there, but we must go and get it. Mercy is "grace in action," grace poured out upon us. When God pours out His grace upon us, this grace is divine mercy. Hence, mercy is grace in action. "That we may obtain mercy, and find grace to help in time of need." Surely, we recognize by now that every moment in the flesh is a time of need. We need something every moment that we are living in this Church Age, and those needs can be met by going to the throne of grace. At this point prayer and the faith-rest technique cross, and the two paths then come together and form a secret and a basis of power which takes us back to the mechanics once more.

Here is the faith-rest technique coming in one direction, and then it bumps into prayer at verse 16. Here is prayer coming in too, and when the two come in together they form once again the mechanics of the faith-rest life. The filling of the Holy Spirit, or spirituality, is the source of power in the Christian life and the faith-rest technique is the means of utilizing that power. There are many problems which are solved by taking them to God in prayer. You see, every time we use I Peter 5:7 ("Casting all your care upon him, for he careth for you") we are actually using the faith-rest technique, but the faith-rest technique is used mechanically with prayer. Perhaps right now you have a problem, a difficulty, some kind of a situation which has been disturbing you. Then here is your answer. Prayer! You go to God in prayer: "Let us come boldly unto the throne of grace." As you go to God in prayer, you take I Peter 5:7 and believe it, which is the faith-rest life. You actually, as the object of your faith, believe I Peter 5:7.

# THE DYNAMICS OF WAITING
## ISAIAH 40

The introduction to Chapter 40 of Isaiah is found at the conclusion of the chapter in verse 29. "He giveth power to the faint; and to them that have no might he increaseth strength." Isaiah was facing a very discouraged crowd, one which was about to go into captivity. They were soon to become the recipients of very heavy judgment. The picture was very black and very dark in many ways. And so the usual thing was happening among the believers of Isaiah's day, just as it happens among believers of this day. Some were "sitting on the panic button" and inviting others to join them. Others were simply singing the blues, discouraged and despondent. In short, they had fainted, an experience which occurs about every other second with believers in our age. We live in a very special age from the standpoint of fainting. Believers do not seem to be able to trust very long when it comes to the problems of life and the adversities, and above all, those moments which cannot be explained, those disheartening circumstances. Hence, the very objective of the Word of God in this passage is to show you that you do not have to be despondent, you do not have to go through life singing the blues, that you do not have to live *on* your emotions and *by* your emotions—up one moment and down the next. Nor do you have to flit around like a bee, trying every little flower for some emotional experience, or trying to find the second, third or fourth blessing—trying to find some super, hyper-spiritual experience which is going to turn the world upside down. God is not giving out any super-duper ecstatic experience to any one person or any small group of people. The Christian way of life belongs to every Christian. If you are a believer in Jesus Christ, "waiting on the Lord" is a principle which belongs to YOU!

Isaiah faced two extremes. He faced the extremes of believers who were discouraged and the extremes of believers who always had a gimmick, who always had some hyper-spiritual way of settling everything. The group who try to agonize themselves into being more spiritual than anyone else. And so we have this wonderful passage which introduces the dynamics of waiting.

We find, first of all, that we have an experience in common. Fainting! We have it today as they had it in that day, for we read in Hebrews 12:3, " 'Keep occupied with him' . . . lest you be wearied and faint in your minds." Now I do not know how many of you are fainting. But if you are, stand by, for the wonderful thing is that you can still hear the Word of God. I know that many of you are carrying tremendous and serious problems on your hearts. I know that many of you are completely frustrated by the human viewpoint of life. I know that many of you are discouraged and many of you have become despondent, you have almost given up, while others of you, recognizing this same condition, are trying to do something about it in your own strength. You are seeking, or perhaps you have found, or perhaps you are practicing some form of sublimation. You have found a substitute. You are not going to be beaten down. You have found some way of finding a little happiness in life. It might be anything from a bottle to some type of intellectual stimulation. And so, you have your kind of sublimation which is going to compensate for you.

Now let us wade through all of this confusion, the turmoil inside of you, the problems in your life, the difficulties which beset, that down-at-the-mouth attitude you have on the inside. Of course, I recognize that by now many of you are excellent poker players. You can sit there and look at me with a straight face and give me that "who me?" look. Yet, you are holding the greatest hand in the world, the promises of God, the techniques of the Bible, the doctrines of Scripture—you have all of these wonderful assets. Or perhaps at this point some of you are cranking out the "sanctified" look, that "this doesn't concern me at all look, because I am above all that." Now let's face it. This is true of all of us. This is true of me. This is true of you. There are times when we faint. There are times when we "throw in the sponge," when we give up, when we are discouraged. And that time has come for many of you this week. So we read in verse 29 something which belongs to us by way of application, even as it belonged to believing Israel in Isaiah's day by way of interpretation. As Isaiah comes to the end of his great message, he says, "He giveth power to the faint."

When God gives power, the only power He can give is

divine power. God's own power! Not human power nor human ability! He did it in the past in Isaiah's day; He has done it since Isaiah's day, and as a matter of fact, even before Isaiah's day. When the Jews had their backs to the wall, as it were, at the Red Sea and were facing certain annihilation, He gave power to the helpless, for Moses had said, "Stand still and see the deliverance of the Lord" (Exodus 14:13). You are helpless, you cannot fight, you cannot struggle, you cannot solve your problem. So stand aside and watch the Lord solve it. There is a principle which I must get over to you and I hope you are tuned in on the right frequency. This principle came from the lips of David as he stood before Goliath and said, "The battle is the Lord's" (I Samuel 17:47).

If you are a believer in Jesus Christ, if you have trusted in Him as your Lord and Saviour, this is not your fight any more—this is the Lord's battle. Therefore, it is most ludicrous, in fact, it becomes the epitome of stupidity for a believer to try to fight the battle when it is the Lord's battle and not yours! The Lord says for you to stand aside and watch Him fight, or as He puts it in the last verse here, "Wait on me." The hardest thing in the Christian life to do is to do nothing! How many times have I talked to many of you personally? I have faced your problems with you. I have listened to the difficulties which befell you. I have been compassionate and sympathetic. Maybe I have shown it and maybe I have not, but deep down inside of me there is a tremendous well of compassion because I know what you are going through and I know what the answer is. So, very often when you get through telling me your problems and your difficulties, I have said, in so many words—"What should you do about it? Do nothing!" By doing nothing I do not mean simply to sit down and contemplate infinity. I do not mean to let your mind go blank and sort of blot yourself out. Nor do I mean to cease from all the normal functions and activities of life. By doing nothing I mean to let go of the problem and trust it to the Lord. As it says here, to "wait on him." And here is the secret: "He giveth power to the faint." He can only give power to the faint; He can only give power to the helpless. God does not help those who help themselves. That is not in the Bible. God helps the helpless! Therefore, since "the battle is the Lord's," since I as a believer belong to Him, since I am helpless and since I have tried to solve my own problems and have constantly run up against a stone wall and have many bumps on the cerebrum to prove it, the thing for me to do is to depend upon Him.

Why, we just barely recognize that we have problems, and we pass out, we faint, we get discouraged. Then we try to detour around the realities of life by some escapism, some sublimation, some something, which will not work. At the other extreme, we just sit down and worry and worry and worry until we become, as believers, the most miserable of creatures. But, "He gives power to the faint, and to them who have NO might, he increases their strength." Listen, God can never help you until you recognize that you are helpless. God cannot help you until you recognize the fact that you cannot do it yourself.

We live in a do-it-yourself generation. But there is one thing you cannot do yourself. You cannot save yourself. You are saved by grace through faith. But even after salvation, you cannot help yourself. The filling of the Spirit does not come by something you do. You cannot do anything—period! You can produce only by the power that He gives. Nothing in the Christian life is generated by your own effort. I have a fine automobile, which I like very much. I am what is known as "a satisfied customer." But in spite of all of the wonderful gadgets, in spite of all of the advantages of this automobile, there is one very definite disadvantage. It must have gasoline. It needs fuel to run. So I have to keep pulling into some gas station every so often, because in spite of the fact that it is a wonderful automobile, it requires gas. The principle of combustion by which it moves requires that certain parts of air and certain parts of gasoline run through the line, drawing them into the carburetor. No matter how great the automobiles are, they all run on the same principle, whether they are large or small, old or new. They all have to have the same thing. Likewise in the spiritual realm it doesn't make any difference whether you are a big person or a little person, old or young, if you are a believer in Jesus Christ, God has given you at the moment of regeneration a spiritual carburetor, and this carburetor runs on God the Holy Spirit! Therefore, here was encouraging news to the believing Jews of that day and should be very encouraging news to you today. If you have come to the end of yourself, if you have faced with Elijah the dried-up brook, if you have come to the place where you realize the situation is hopeless and you are helpless to cope with it, then you are in a position, most grand beyond expression, to recognize that only God can help you. If you begin to realize this through the pressures of experience, or by a much easier method, by believing the Word of God, you are in a position to have the very power of God in your life, because He gives power to the helpless, He gives power to the fainting.

In verse 30 we see an illustration from athletics. The Hebrew says, "Even the athletes shall faint." No matter how well a man is prepared, he sometimes faints. There are times when he gives out, no matter how strong he is. ". . . and the young men shall utterly fall." No matter how fine athletes are, there are times when they faint and when they fall. "But . . ." Even though we faint, grow weary and fall, there is hope, there is a promise. "But they that wait upon the Lord. . . ." Verse 31 goes back to the spiritual principle, which we must understand before we get back in the 40th Chapter of Isaiah. How do you wait on the Lord? Let us look more closely at the word "wait," which could be translated "trust" or "faith."

There are actually five or six Hebrew words for faith. One Hebrew word translated "faith" is found in Genesis 15:6. This is the Hebrew word "amen." It means to use God as a prop; to use God as a foundation, to lean on Him. Then there is a Hebrew word translated "faith" or "trust" in Psalm 37:3. This Hebrew word was originally used of two wrestlers grappling, when finally one of them picks the other up and slams him down to the ground. From this the word eventually came to mean "pick up your troubles and problems and slam them on the Lord," and therefore, became another word for "trust." Then, a word used in Psalm 57:1, was used to "flee as a bunny," as a rabbit would flee from a large, vicious animal. The rabbit does not stop to fight with a snarling, snapping predator hot on its trail. He knows who would win, so he flees. But his enemy is too much for him, and as he is about to faint, he suddenly discovers a rock with a crack in it, or, to use the Biblical term, a cleft. So the little bunny hops into the cleft, goes back in as far as possible, and he is safe. This word, first used for a bunny running away from a big animal and finding safety in the cleft of a rock, actually meant "to flee as a rabbit in the cleft of a rock." Again, it is a word for faith. It means to hide in the cleft of The Rock, Christ Jesus, where nothing can touch you.

Another word, found in Job 13:15, means to trust in extreme pain. Even though you are utterly and totally miserable, or in extreme pain, you have confidence of deliverance. It came to mean faith, too. But the Holy Spirit does not use any of these words in this verse. There is one other word, translated "wait," which is not a bad translation, although it does not convey the whole idea. The word was originally used of making rope. There is first just a litttle strand, which is easy to break. This is the "fainter." But as this little strand is woven in with other strands, it becomes a rope which cannot be broken. Hence, this word meant to be a strand twisted into a great rope and therefore made strong, and it came to mean "trust." Those who *wait* on the Lord are "those who keep on trusting the Lord." Even though they are weak little strands, those who keep on trusting the Lord become a gigantic, powerful rope which nothing can break. It is interesting to note that in the Old Testament every time you find the word "faith" or the word "trust," it is one of these five Hebrew words, but in every passage there is a little different emphasis. In the passage before us "wait" should be translated, "But they who habitually trust the Lord. . . ." "They who keep on trusting the Lord in spite of all difficulties, in spite of the hopelessness of the situation, those who keep on using the faith-rest technique. . . ."

Now what is going to happen to them? The word "renew" is a very poor translation. The idea is not renewing strength as your physical strength is renewed. God is not talking about human strength at all. He is talking about divine strength. It should be, literally, "They who keep on trusting the Lord shall *exchange* their strength." The Hebrew word for "exchange" meant to "exchange your human strength for divine strength." To turn in your strength, which at best is very weak, and to get back divine strength. When we say, "Lord, I can't do it," the Lord answers, "I will solve the problem, I will give you the strength, I will provide everything necessary for you to meet this difficult problem in your life." But, I want you to notice, there is no exchange of human strength for divine strength until there is a constant trusting the Lord. This is not a verse for sprinters.

I wonder how many of you are sprinters? Are you the kind of a person who, when there is a great emotional appeal, gets all worked up and you vow to yourself that when you get out of that service, you are going to do great things for God? So you move out, all a rosy glow, to conquer the world! You are going to do great things for Jesus Christ—and then, the tumult and the shouting die. The emotion ebbs away, as it always does, and what does it leave? An empty shell. Just someone who said words, "I am going to do this and this and that." You were all fired up emotionally, but not spiritually. When the emotion fades, which was your crutch, the steam is all gone. You have no impetus with which to follow through. Your dependence was upon being stirred up. Now, please do not think that I am condemning emotions, because we are all emotional, we all have emotions, just do not *depend* upon your emotions. You must depend upon the Holy Spirit, and upon the Word. Depend upon the things that are real, those things which will keep you moving, moving, moving.

Now, what is a sprinter? A sprinter is one who believes for a few minutes, or while his emotions are aroused, but when the emotions ebb away, he stops believing, he stops moving. And so the poor old preacher has to start to shovel in the coal and fire up the boiler again, the same way he did it before, and pretty soon he has a congregation who is either way down, or aroused emotionally, with very few lasting results. But this is bound to be the result of a ministry dedicated to sad stories, thin devotions and other impotent substitutes for the teaching of the Word of God, which we find so prevalent in the ministry today.

But this verse says, "The power of God does not come in fits and starts, it does not come in spurts and stops; the power of God is a steady, continuous energy which is not dependent upon emotion, rationalism or anything else. It depends upon believing the Word of God! Waiting on the Lord, habitual waiting on the Lord ! Believing the Word of God no matter how tough things get, no matter how prosperous things are. I want you to ask yourself a question very frankly at this point, "Do I believe the Word of God when things are tough? Do I keep on believing the Word of God, or do I have to be aroused emotionally? Do I have to be stirred up and fired up?" Do you move by fits and starts, or do you move continuously—steady, stable, powerful, producing dynamic things for the Lord?

"They that wait upon the Lord shall exchange their strength." They turn in their old miserable, puny, human strength for marvelous, wonderful divine strength. And what is the result?

They fly—"they shall mount up with wings as eagles; and they shall run and not be weary. . . ." They keep on moving; they do not run out of gas; they keep running through everything. Nothing can stop them! "They keep on walking," the Hebrew says, "and do not faint." Now, isn't this a wonderful life? The life of waiting on the Lord; the dynamics of waiting on Him. Keeping on trusting Him no matter how black the picture is, no matter how dark the situation or how great the adversity. To keep on trusting Him; to keep on believing Him! The 40th Chapter of Isaiah is a passage which says, in effect, "It pays to wait on the Lord; it pays to keep on trusting Him. He is the only one whom you can keep trusting and know that everything is going to work out."

Now, look back at *Verse 12*, where we shall see how it pays to wait on Him.

> Who hath measured the waters in the hollow of his hand, and meted out heaven with the span, and comprehended the dust of the earth in a measure, and weighed the mountains in scales, and the hills in a balance?

It pays to wait on Him because He has the *power* to execute the impossible. This verse indicates something of His omnipotence, for "measuring the waters in the hollow of his hand" speaks of great power. God, the Lord Jesus Christ, can measure all of the waters, all of the seas in the world in the palm of His hand. But, more than that, He meted out the heavens with His little finger. The word "span" means "little finger."

A cluster of stars called the Andromeda Nebulae gives us some idea of the vastness of our universe. I use the Andromeda Nebulae as an example because this is as far as the human eye can see. If you look up at the Andromeda Nebulae tonight, the light which reaches your eye will have left that particular series of stars one million, six hundred thousand years ago! Now, we measure space, as far as the universe is concerned, by the distance light can travel in one year. We have discovered that light travels about six trillion miles in one year. Now you can figure how far you are from the Andromeda Nebulae. So if light can travel six trillion miles in one year, and it takes one million, six hundred thousand years for the light to come from Andromeda Nebulae to this earth, that gives you a rough idea of distance in outer space.

Man talks about his fantastic achievements in outer space; he is awed by such things as "Sputnik." Why, that should be called "Sputter-nik," when compared to the vastness of God's handiwork! Man fiddles around here a little bit, he uses a principle of gravity plus a rocket and he gets something out into space that moves around, and—so what? How far out in space is it? Just step out one night and look at the Andromeda Nebulae, the light of which left there one million, six hundred thousand years ago, traveling at the speed of six trillion miles a year. And yet the Andromeda Nebulae is merely a very close-in set of stars. Beyond the Andromeda Nebulae are millions and billions and trillions of stars, and they have been there for a long time. We can see the light through the telescope, and in some cases it took that light billions of years to come. And with His little finger Jesus Christ put the whole thing out there.

Now, I want to ask you a question. If Jesus Christ can move His little finger and put into existence billions and billions of stars and millions of galaxies, billions of light years apart, I wonder, do you think He can handle your problems? That was all finger work. Do you suppose He can meet the needs of your life? What is the point of verse 12? It pays to wait on Him. It pays to keep on trusting Him. Why? Because He is powerful; He can take care of your problems; He can handle the situation.

*Verse 13.* It pays to wait on the Lord because He has revealed a way to wait on Him. He is the Revealer. "Who hath directed the Spirit of the Lord (God the Holy Spirit), or being his counsellor hath taught Him?" God the Holy Spirit is the teacher of the Word of God. And not only has He the power to do those things, such as solving our problems and meeting our needs, He has even revealed to us the way in which we latch on to this power. It is through none other than the faith-rest technique, the moment-by-moment Sabbath, which is the means revealed by God the Holy Spirit whereby we claim this infinite power for every need in our life. So, in verse 13, what we actually have, in effect, is that He has provided the Holy Spirit, and the Holy Spirit reveals through the Word of God the way to wait on Him.

In verse 12—it pays to wait on Him; He has the power: Omnipotence.

In verse 13—it pays to wait on Him; He presents the method: The Revealer.

In verse 14—it pays to wait on Him; He knows best. And here is a further principle—His omniscience!

*Verse 14.* "With whom took he (the Lord Jesus) counsel? Who instructed the Lord Jesus and taught the Lord Jesus in the path of judgment? And who taught the Lord Jesus knowledge and showed to the Lord Jesus the way of understanding?" No one! Why? Because He is omniscient! Therefore, to wait upon the Lord, is to wait upon the One who always knows best. This is why the best thing you can do, in many cases, is NOTHING! But by doing nothing, I do not mean to set up an experiential vacuum in your life. I do mean to set up an experiential positive, pulsating, moment-by-moment believing. Every time your heart pumps you should also be pumping faith toward Him. Believing, believing, believing, regardless of what happens. Believing even to the very place where Job came when he said, "Though he slay me, yet will I trust him" (Job 13:15). That is waiting on the Lord. That is the moment-by-moment Sabbath, and that is the faith-rest technique carried out to the finest degree.

It is easy to trust the Lord when everything is going right. It is easy to trust the Lord when you have been stirred up emotionally. It is easy to trust the Lord when everything is going your way. But, do you trust the Lord when the picture is black? If you get to the place where you think you do, then take heed, for God is going to test that position! There are believers who this very week have been tested. God has said, "Do you really trust Me? Do you really believe My Word?" And just as you begin to think you do, and the situation is clearing God says, "Now, I am going to blank out this situation; I am going to make it look hopeless and black. Do you still believe Me?"

Listen, if the situation around you is absolutely dark and hopeless today, is the same Lord on the other side of the darkness? Can you look through the darkness and see Him? Can you look through the darkness and the hopelessness of your situation and see His Word? Has He changed on the other side of your adverse circumstances? No, He hasn't changed! "Jesus Christ, the same yesterday, today and forever" (Hebrews 13:8). He will never change. Therefore, He is just as faithful today as He was the day before, as He was in Isaiah's day, as He was in Moses' day, and He will continue to be just as faithful. He will continue to tap His foot just waiting to bless you (Isaiah 30:18). Yes, the Lord is waiting, too. He is waiting for us to trust Him. Actually, He is waiting for us to wait on Him, so that He no longer has to wait to bless us. So He puts up the hopeless picture for us where everything is black and despairing, yet on the other side of the picture is the same faithful Lord. And He says, "Trust Me through this! Trust Me in the midst of this! Believe Me! Believe the Word!" As long as you refuse to believe Him, the situation will continue to be bad. There will be no peace or stability until you learn to trust Him. Waiting upon the Lord is the greatest economy of time.

We have seen His omnipotence, His omniscience and immutability. Now we have His sovereignty.

*Verse 15.* "Look! Behold, the nations are as a drop of a bucket, and are counted as the small dust of the balance: behold he taketh up the isles as a very little thing." Did you ever step back and look at the nations of the world? Ruling them would be quite a chore for us. But ruling all of the nations in the world is no more a burden than carrying a drop of water in a bucket for the Lord Jesus Christ. It is that easy for Him. It is no harder for the Lord to rule over the nations of the earth than to put a little dust on a scale. It pays to wait upon the One whose decisions are wiser than our decisions. And our decisions are suspended by faith as we wait on Him. Yet instead, our tendency is more often to try this first or do that, or to move somewhere to escape the hopeless situation here, or to insist on a decision right now—we just must do something! But the more we *do,* the more we tangle up the situation. The less we try and the more we trust, the quicker can God bring the solution. And the greater will be the blessing all of the time, even before the solution breaks.

*Verse 16.* "And Lebanon is not sufficient to burn, nor the beasts thereof sufficient for a burnt offering." In other words, when they worshipped the Lord, they needed wood to burn. In that day the sacrifice was the burnt offering. But they could burn all the wood and sacrifice all the animals for a burnt offering, and it still would not be sufficient to express how wonderful He is. The glory of the Lord Jesus Christ is so great that there is nothing in human life to express it, not even burning the forests, nor offering all the animals.

*Verse 17.* He goes on to say, "All nations before him are as nothing; and they are counted to him less than nothing, and vanity." Why? He has just said in verse 15, "Behold, the nations are as a drop of a bucket, and are counted as the small dust of the balance; behold, he taketh up the isles as a very little thing." He can just pick up an island, it is nothing to Him. He doesn't even have to move His finger. He can pick up an isle and move it out, as He did once in the last century with Krakatoa.

*Verse 18.* "To whom then will ye liken God? or what likeness will ye compare unto him?" Who can compare with the Lord? The question is rhetorical, for no one can compare with Him! Since no one can compare with the Lord, why trust anyone less than the Lord and what He has given to us—His Word? Do you know anyone who could compare with the Lord?

"To whom then will ye liken God?" Or, "what likeness will you compare unto him?" Here is what these people had been doing. They began by taking some beautiful images and overlaying them with gold.

*Verse 19.* "The workman melteth a graven image, and the goldsmith spreadeth it over with gold, and casteth silver chains." He makes an idol; he calls it God. Who made that idol? Man made it! What he makes with his hands, he calls God. If man fashions something with his hands and calls it God, what is man worshipping? He is worshipping that which he has made. In the last half of the verse is a most beautiful twist of sarcasm: "and he casteth silver chains." They had difficulty balancing these idols of gold. This was a great problem. Almost every great idol in the ancient world had some kind of support to keep it from falling over. And they called this idol God, and trusted it, and waited on it!

Now, what are YOU waiting on? What are YOU trusting in? We have our idols today, of gold and silver. The silver chains speak of the fact that they had to anchor these idols to the walls to keep them from falling flat. Are you waiting for or trusting in something that falls flat? Money? Some person? Some thing? Some desire? Something you may already have? What are you leaning on? You may laugh at these people because they made something with their hands out of gold and attached it to the wall with a chain so that the god wouldn't fall—a god which couldn't even hold itself up. They trusted in that! Listen, how many times have you trusted something that is just as foolish? If you are trusting in your money, if you are trusting in some person, if you are trusting in some situation, you are just as stupid as the people here who said, "this is God," and then had to chain it to the wall to keep it from falling flat.

*Verse 20.* "He that is so impoverished that he hath no oblation chooseth a tree that will not rot. . . ." After awhile he runs out of gold, and he needs another god, a new idol. He runs out into the forest and, as it says here, he looks up a piece of wood that will not rot. Now, isn't this amazing? This is just about as bright as some believers are today. He is going to trust in a piece of wood that doesn't rot. Now, how about that? A piece of wood that rots—oh no he couldn't trust that! It rots and disappears. But an idol out of a piece of wood that doesn't rot, a god he has fashioned with his own hands, this is going to help him with the situation—! This piece of wood that doesn't rot cannot help any more than what you and I, as believers, often lean upon. And notice this, would you, please: "he seeketh unto him a cunning workman to prepare a graven image that shall not be moved." But the Hebrew says, literally, "a graven image that shall not fall over." If they made an image out of wood, they had to make it so that the bottom was heavier than the top so it would not fall over, which required a "cunning workman." Therefore, after he fashions it very cunningly so it won't fall over, what happens? Everyone bows before it and says, "I trust you, Oh idol . . . 'Oh Zeus,' 'Oh Aphrodite,' 'Oh Athene;' help me with my problem." My problem is one of love, so I form a beautiful woman and call her Aphrodite. My problem is wisdom, so I make another figure and call this one Athene. My problem is the need of power, so I fashion a man and call him Zeus or Hercules, and I get a cunning workman to do it so Zeus or Aphrodite, or what have you, doesn't fall flat on his or her face while I am in the middle of trusting him or her. Now, isn't this clever? About as sensible as many believers are today, as sensible as any believer is who is trusting in anything beside the Word of God.

What is this passage saying to you and to me? Wait on the

Lord! Keep trusting the Lord! How do we do that today? We have the complete canon of Scripture, but you must know it. You must *know* the promises of His Word, then *believe* them. Anything else you are trusting for your security, or your blessing, or for anything in life is useless. I wonder how many people in the world today worship that which they have made with their own hands? They call it money!

Continuing in *Verse 22.* "It is he that sitteth upon the circle of the earth, and the inhabitants thereof are as grasshoppers. . . ." The earth is said to be a circle, a ball, or actually a sphere. "He stretcheth out the heavens as gauze, or like curtains. . . ." And he continues on down the chapter to say that nothing is planted unless He permits it and nothing is sown without his laws.

*Verse 25.* There is nothing equal to the Holy One, who is the Lord Jesus Christ. "Just look up toward heaven," he says, "look at the vast expanse of the universe." "Lift up your eyes on high, and behold who hath created these things" (*verse 26*). Who has created the universe?

> Colossians 1:16 . . . Jesus Christ
> John 1:3 . . . Jesus Christ
> Hebrews 1:10 . . . Jesus Christ

Jesus Christ created all these things. "It is he," the Hebrew says, "that bringeth out their host by number." All these millions of galaxies He brought out and knows how many. He calls them all by names. Again we see His omniscience. "By the greatness of his might, for that he is strong in power; not one faileth," or literally, "not one of these stars is missing." Isn't that amazing? Billions and quadrillions and infinite numbers of light years away there are stars which are hundreds and thousands of times larger than the earth, and they are still there. He has not lost one yet.

Now if the Lord Jesus Christ created this vast expanse of the universe, if these billions and trillions of large stars and galaxies move around at rapid rates of speed and not one is missing, if God, the Lord Jesus, can keep track of all of this vast universe, He can also keep track of my problems. Not one sparrow falls to the ground without His knowledge. God, who is interested in these tremendous universes and galaxies, is interested in you and in me. He is interested in your problems and mine. If He has yet to lose the first star, then you can be sure He will not forget you. He demands only one thing from you as His child—wait on Him! Believe, believe, believe! Keep on believing the Word of God, no matter what happens, no matter what the difficulties, no matter how adverse the circumstances.

> Hebrews 11:6: "But without faith it is impossible to please him. . . ."
> II Corinthians 5:7: "For we walk by faith, not by sight."

These sermons were preached by Rev. Robert B. Thieme, Jr., and transcribed from tape recordings.

They have been reproduced for the express purpose of bringing honor and glory to the Person of our Saviour, the Lord Jesus Christ.